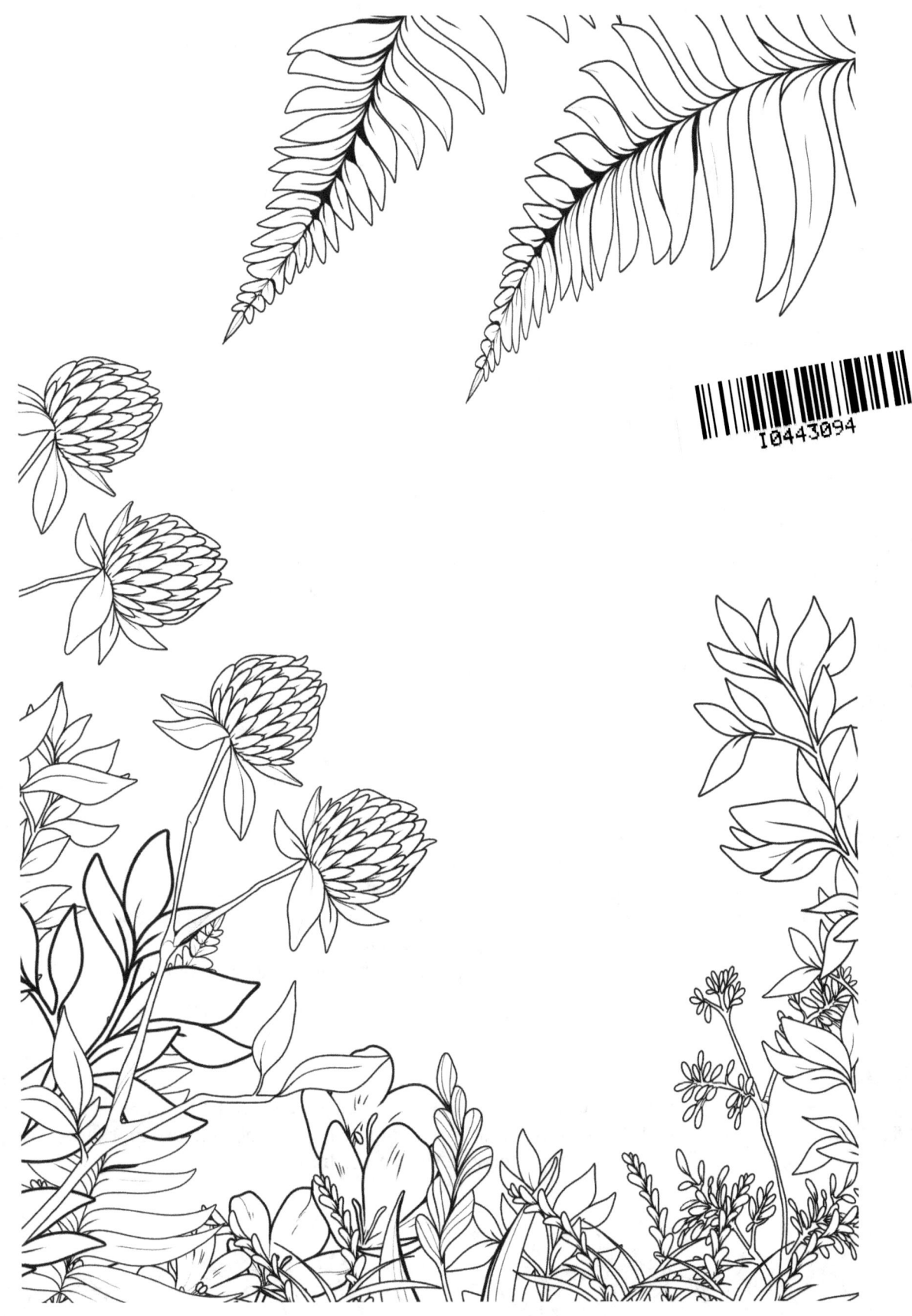

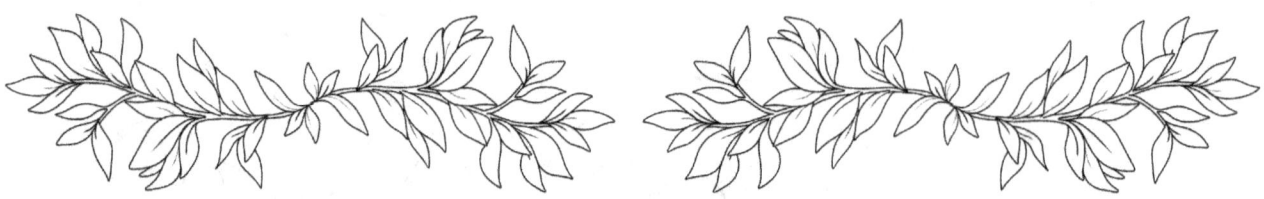

INTRODUCTION

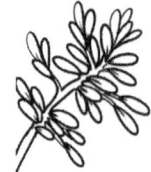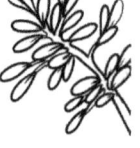

Thank you for your purchase of Calm Coloring: An Animal Colouring Book.

This book is my first completed, published project.
My goal throughout it's creation was to create something which I felt was identifiable to myself, stylewise. I feel as if I achieved this without a lot of outside influence.
The entire project was intended to help me while I was feeling anxious, needed time to myself to focus on something different and let my brain calm down for a while. My initial intention was never to make a colouring book, it was later on when I decided to colour one of the images, that I thought that the format may help people in the same way that it helped me.

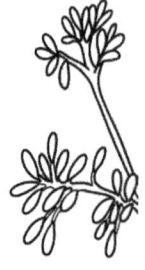

My only goal at this point is that this book helps you find a few minutes, maybe a few hours, to relax and not focus on your worries for a while.

--

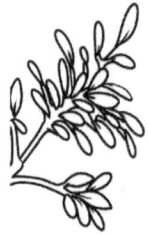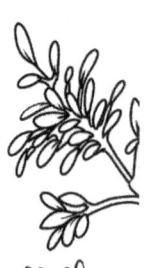

After this page, you will find an eclectic collection of creature drawn in my personal illustrative style.
A few images were experimental, each containing different varied levels of detail with the intent to hopefully be more welcoming and accomodating to people of any experience levels.
A few designs are left customizable so that you may add your own patterns prior to colouring if you wish.

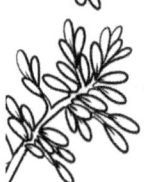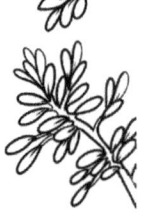

--

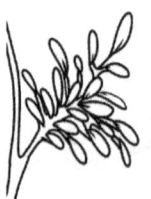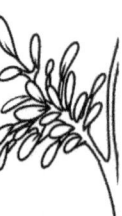

After every page which contains an illustration, there is a bleed page, added with the intent to hopefully soak up some spread of ink, if you choose to use markers or an otherwise similar medium.

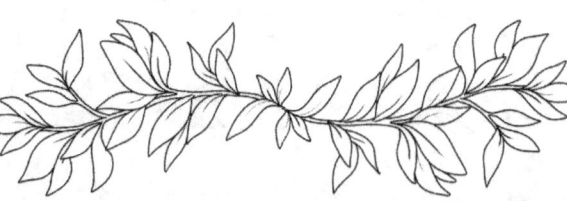

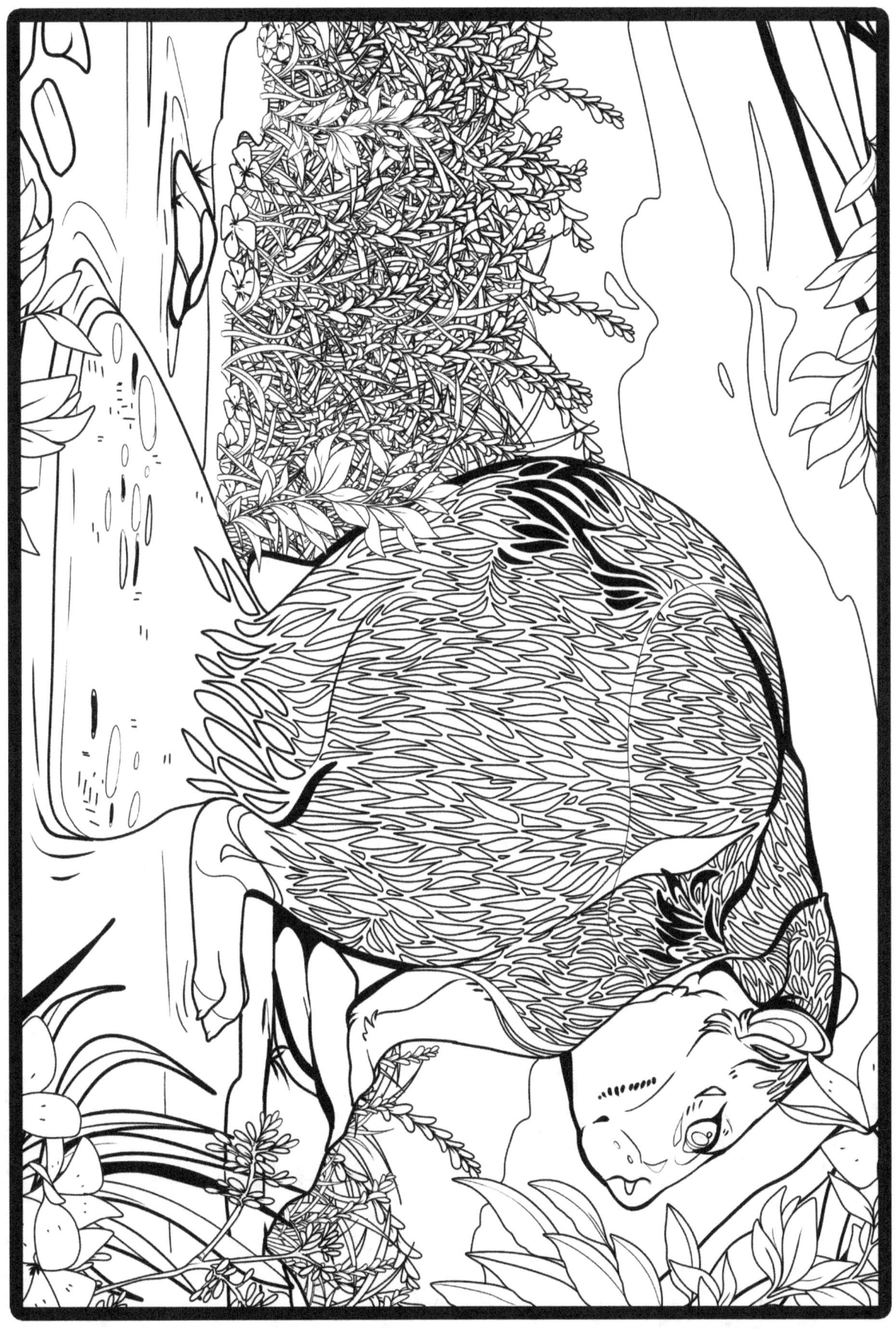

Bleed Page

This page exists to hopefully absorb any leakage of marker ink

Bleed Page

This page exists to
hopefully absorb any
leakage of marker ink

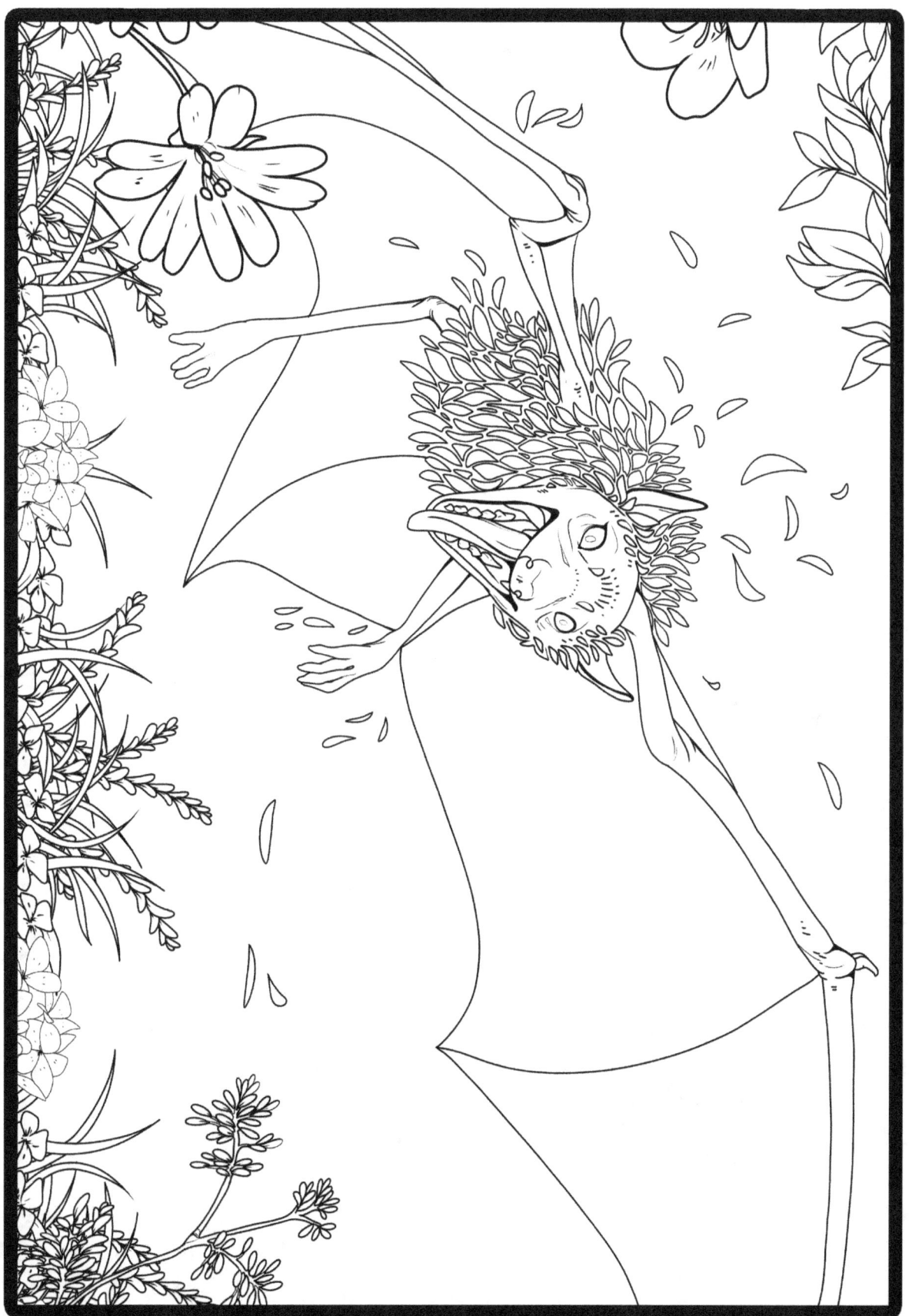

Bleed Page

This page exists to
hopefully absorb any
leakage of marker ink

Bleed Page

This page exists to hopefully absorb any leakage of marker ink

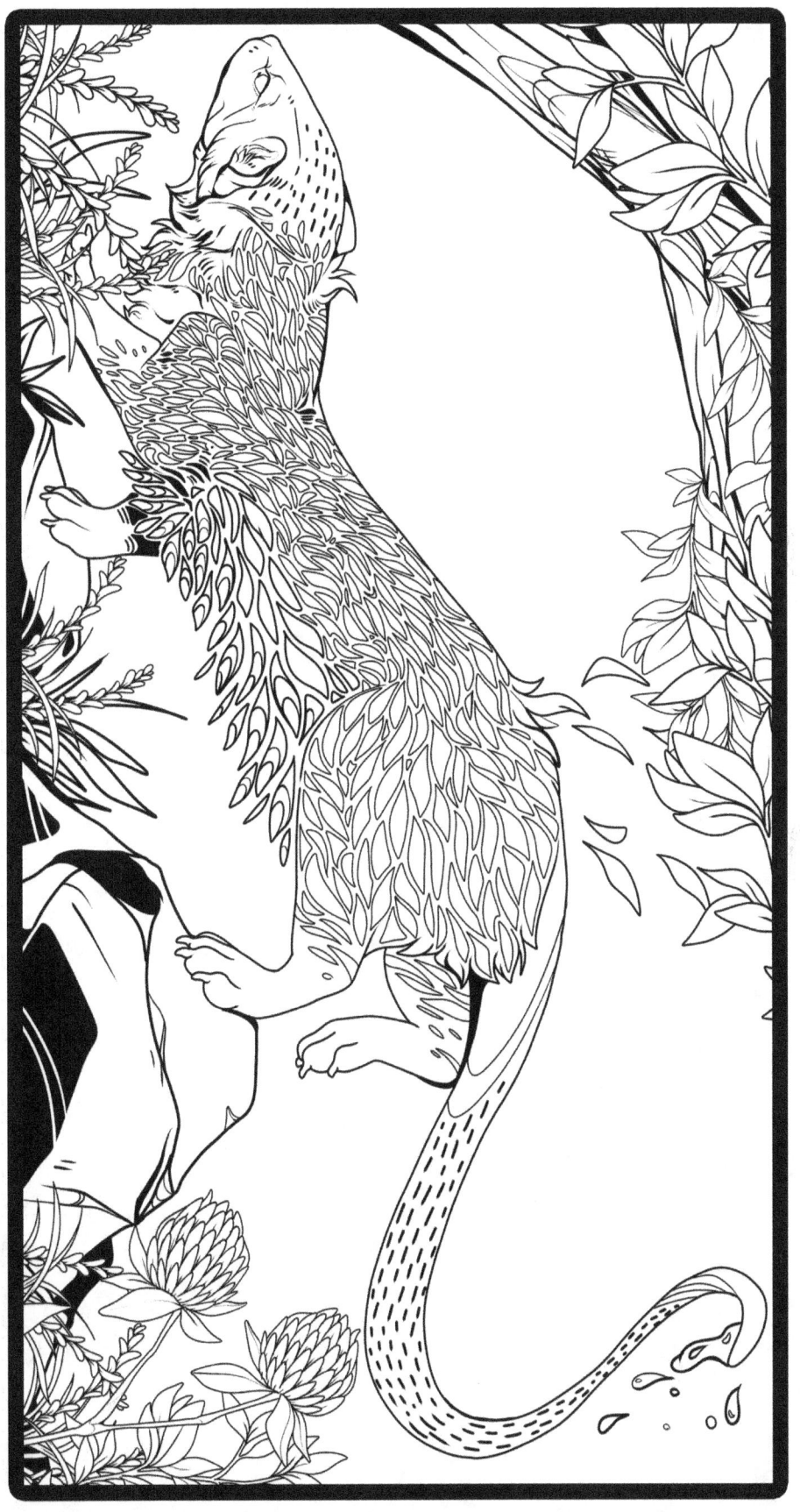

Bleed Page

This page exists to hopefully absorb any leakage of marker ink

Bleed Page

This page exists to hopefully absorb any leakage of marker ink

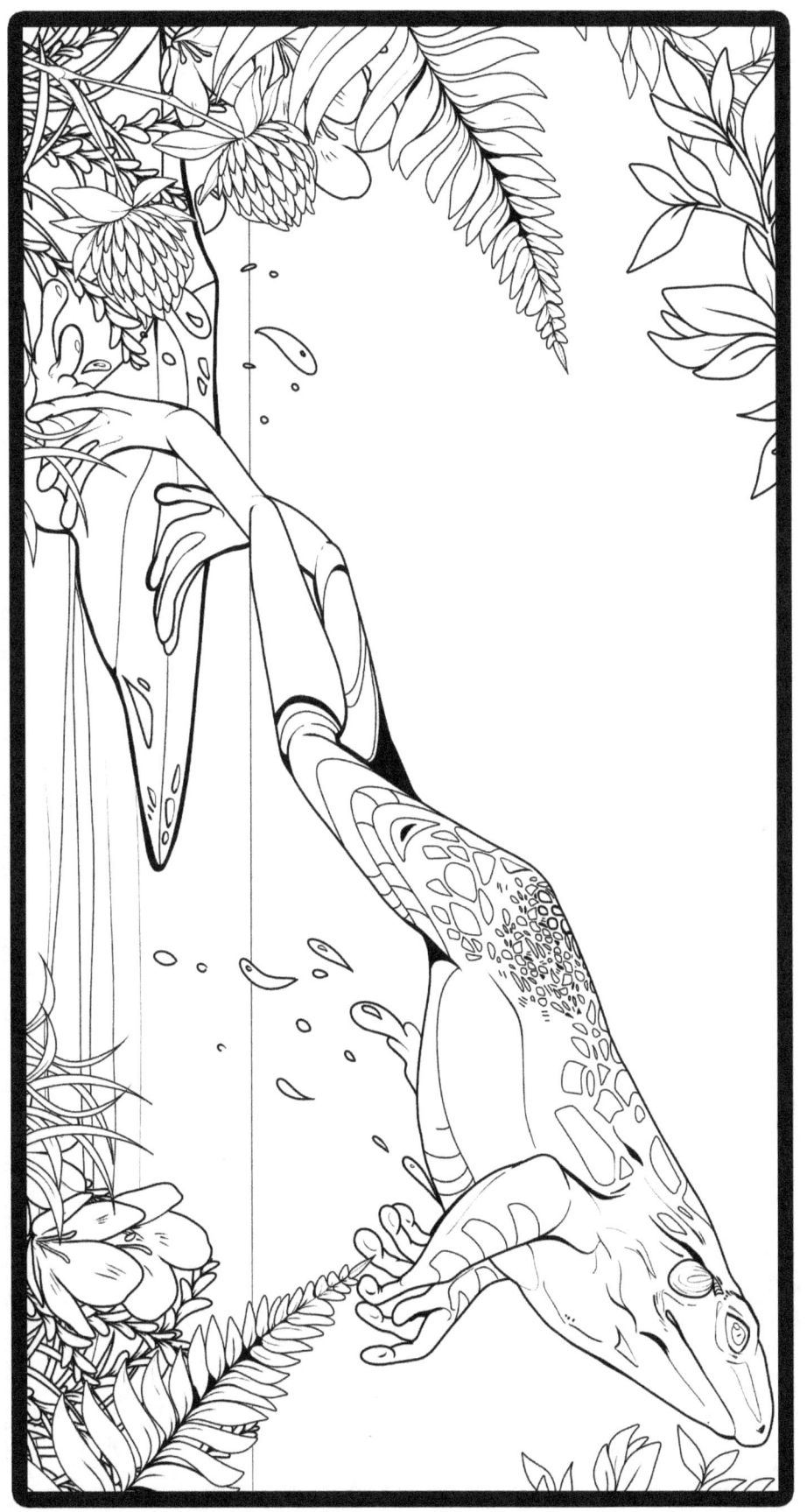

Bleed Page

This page exists to
hopefully absorb any
leakage of marker ink

Bleed Page

This page exists to hopefully absorb any leakage of marker ink

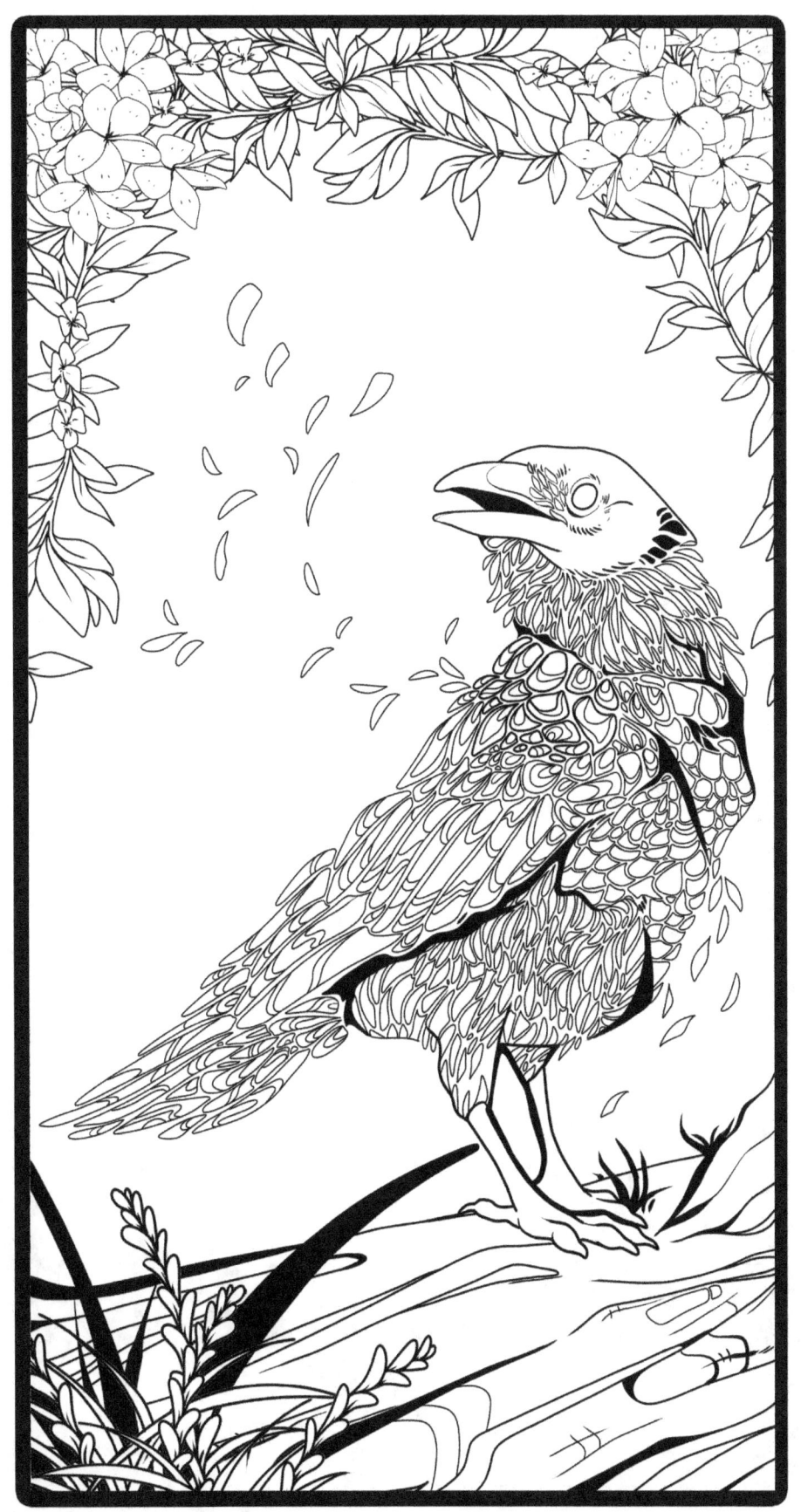

Bleed Page

This page exists to hopefully absorb any leakage of marker ink

Bleed Page

This page exists to hopefully absorb any leakage of marker ink

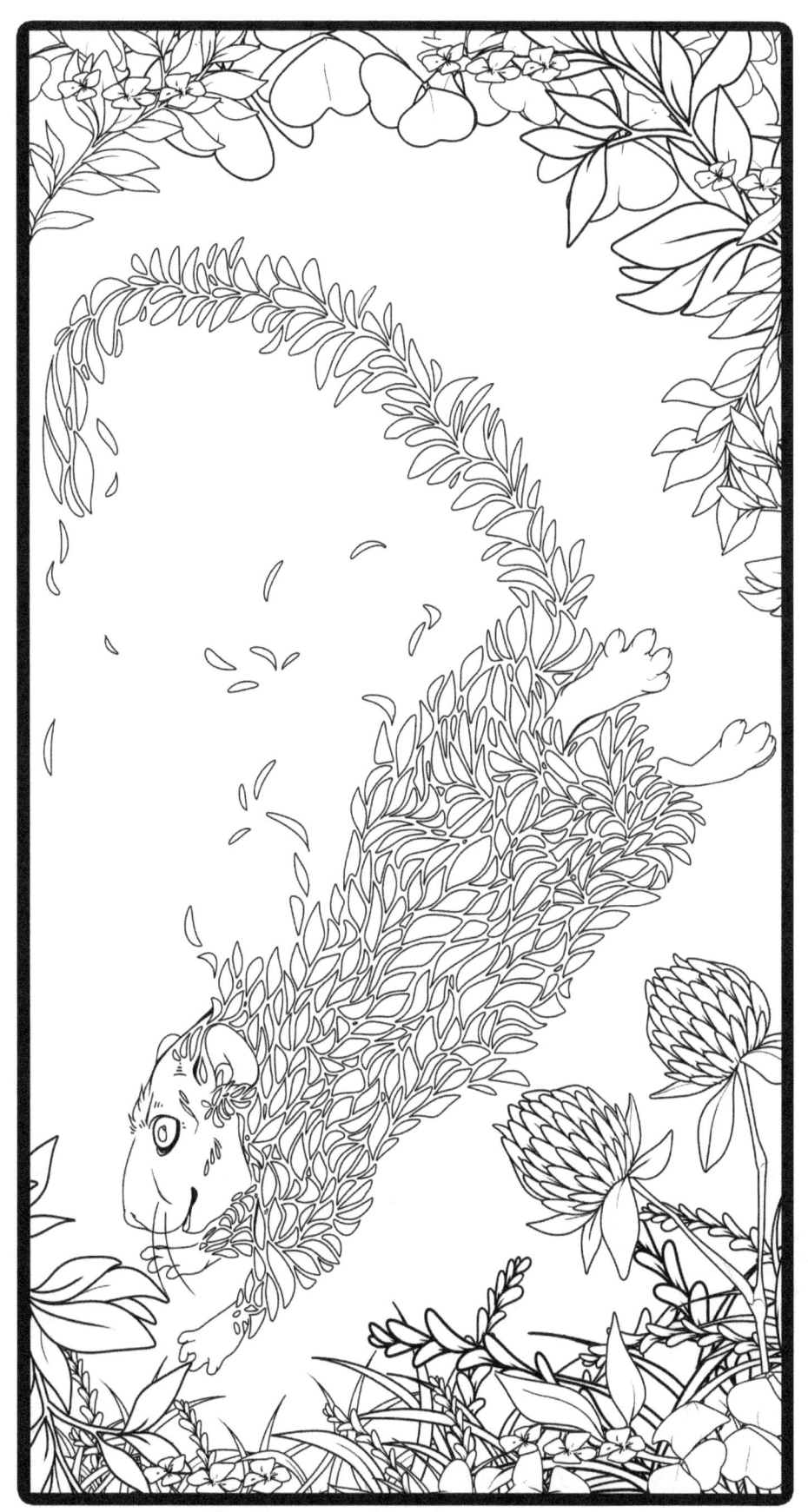

Bleed Page

This page exists to hopefully absorb any leakage of marker ink

Bleed Page

This page exists to
hopefully absorb any
leakage of marker ink

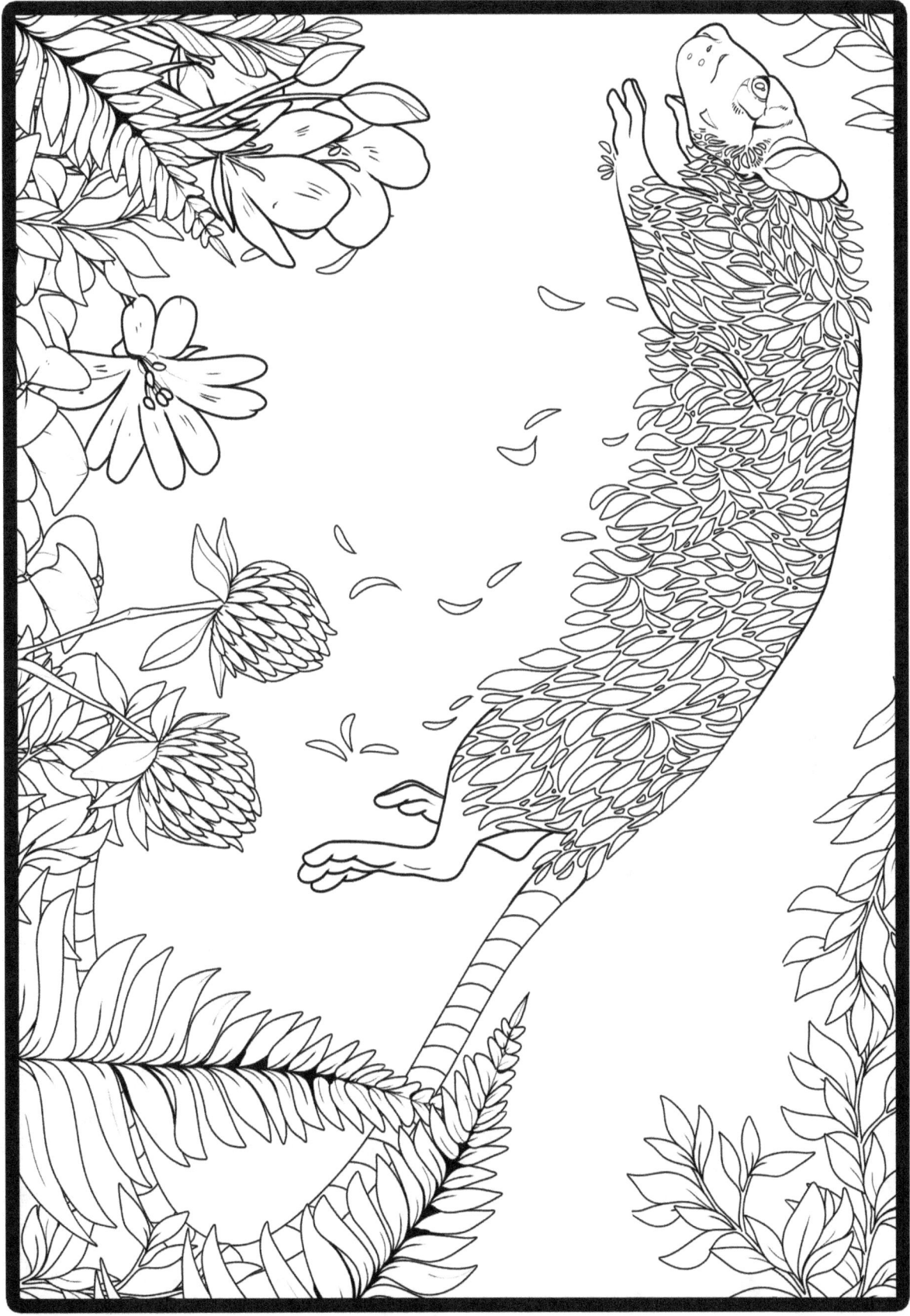

Bleed Page

This page exists to hopefully absorb any leakage of marker ink

Bleed Page

This page exists to hopefully absorb any leakage of marker ink

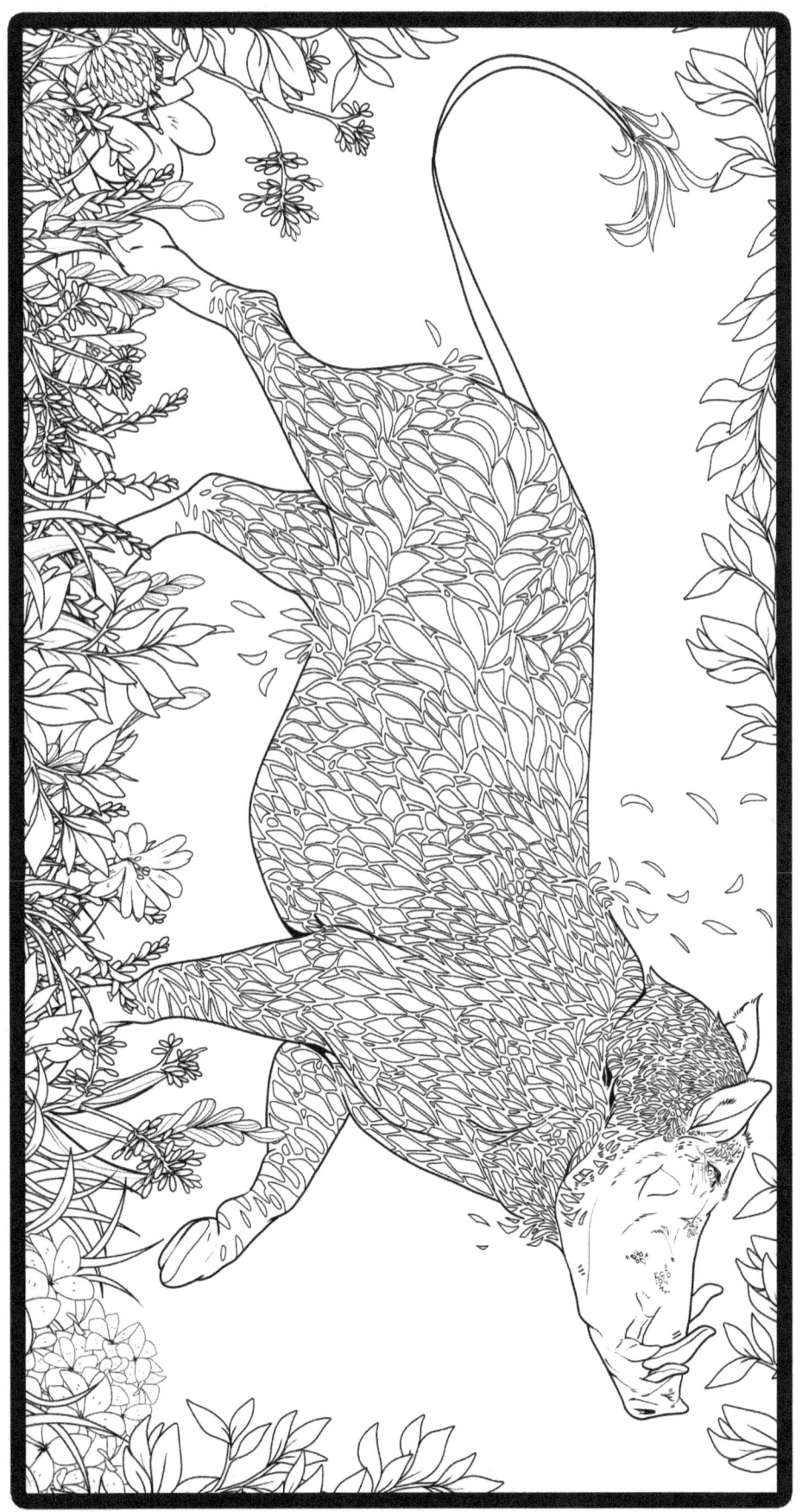

Bleed Page

This page exists to hopefully absorb any leakage of marker ink

Bleed Page

This page exists to hopefully absorb any leakage of marker ink

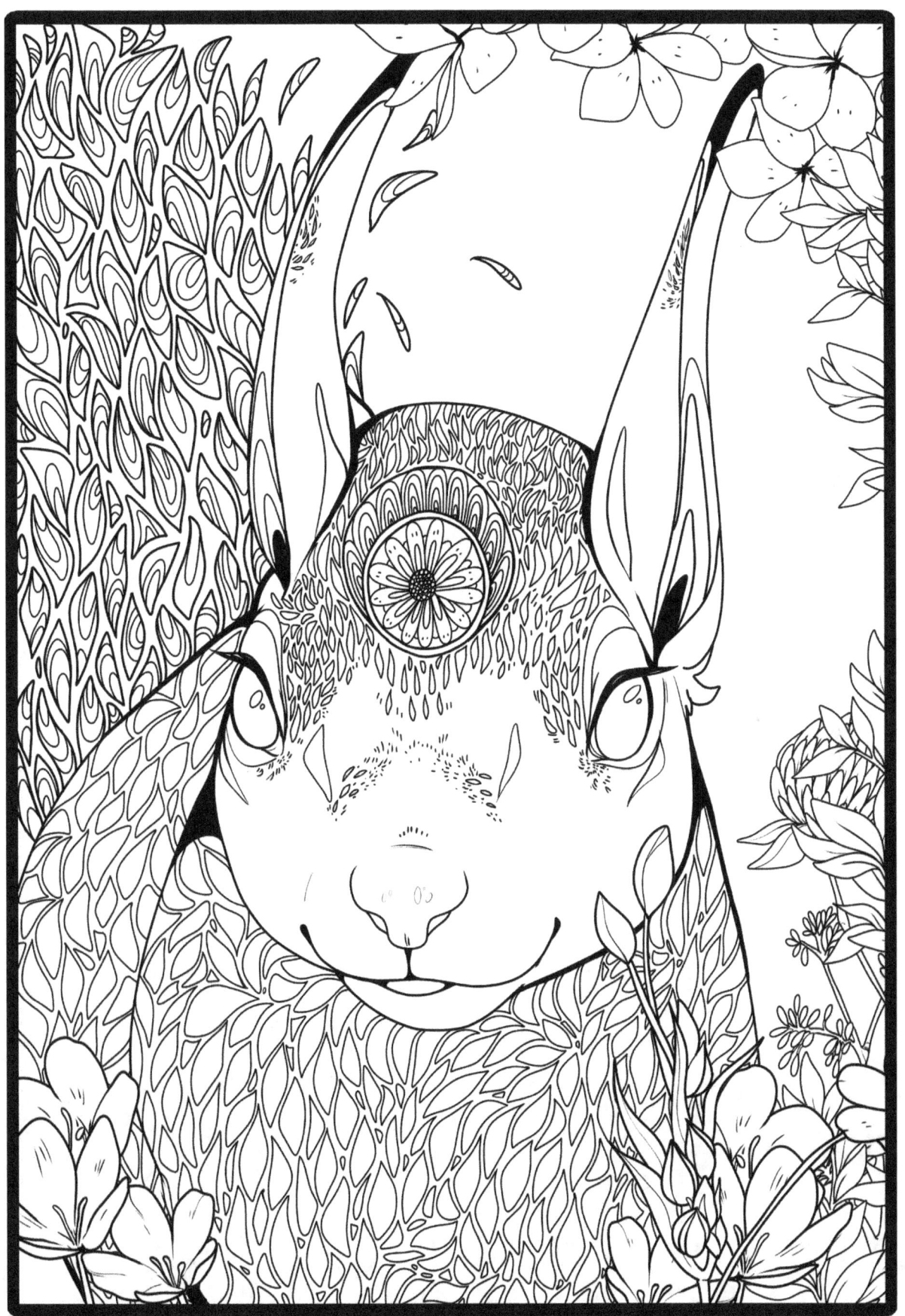

Bleed Page

This page exists to hopefully absorb any leakage of marker ink

Bleed Page

This page exists to hopefully absorb any leakage of marker ink

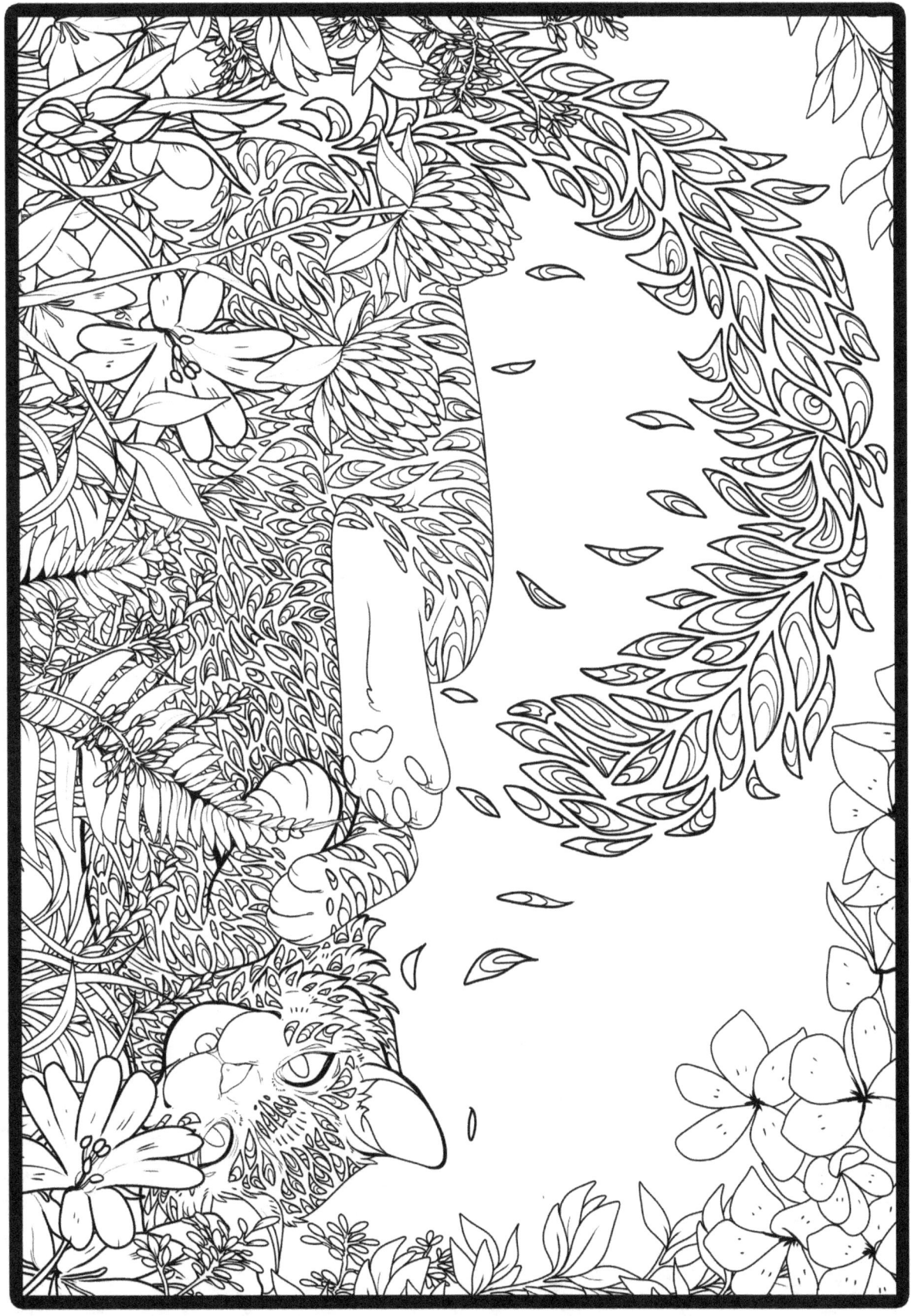

Bleed Page

This page exists to hopefully absorb any leakage of marker ink

Bleed Page

This page exists to hopefully absorb any leakage of marker ink

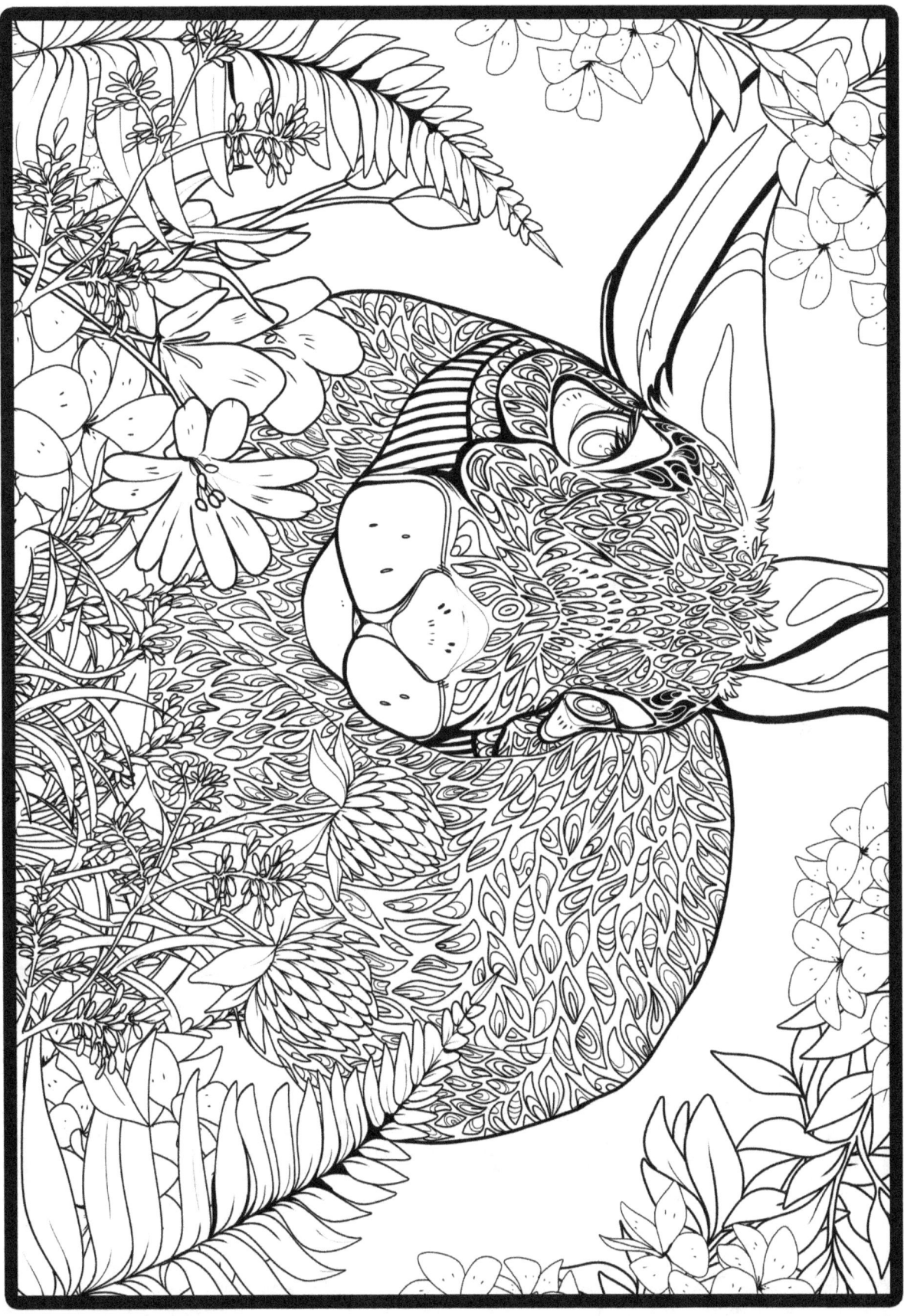

Bleed Page

This page exists to
hopefully absorb any
leakage of marker ink

Bleed Page

This page exists to
hopefully absorb any
leakage of marker ink

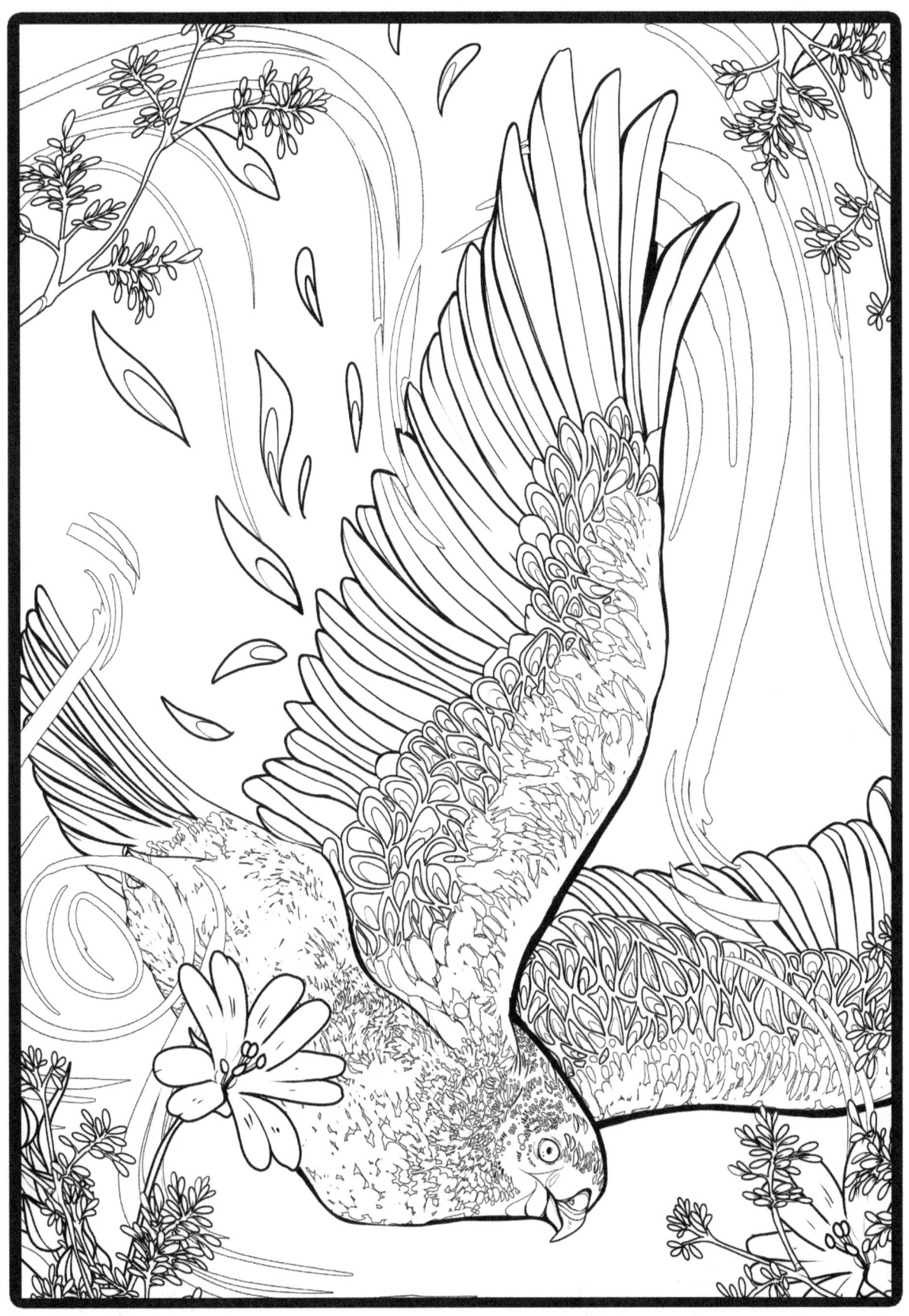

Bleed Page

This page exists to hopefully absorb any leakage of marker ink

Bleed Page

This page exists to
hopefully absorb any
leakage of marker ink

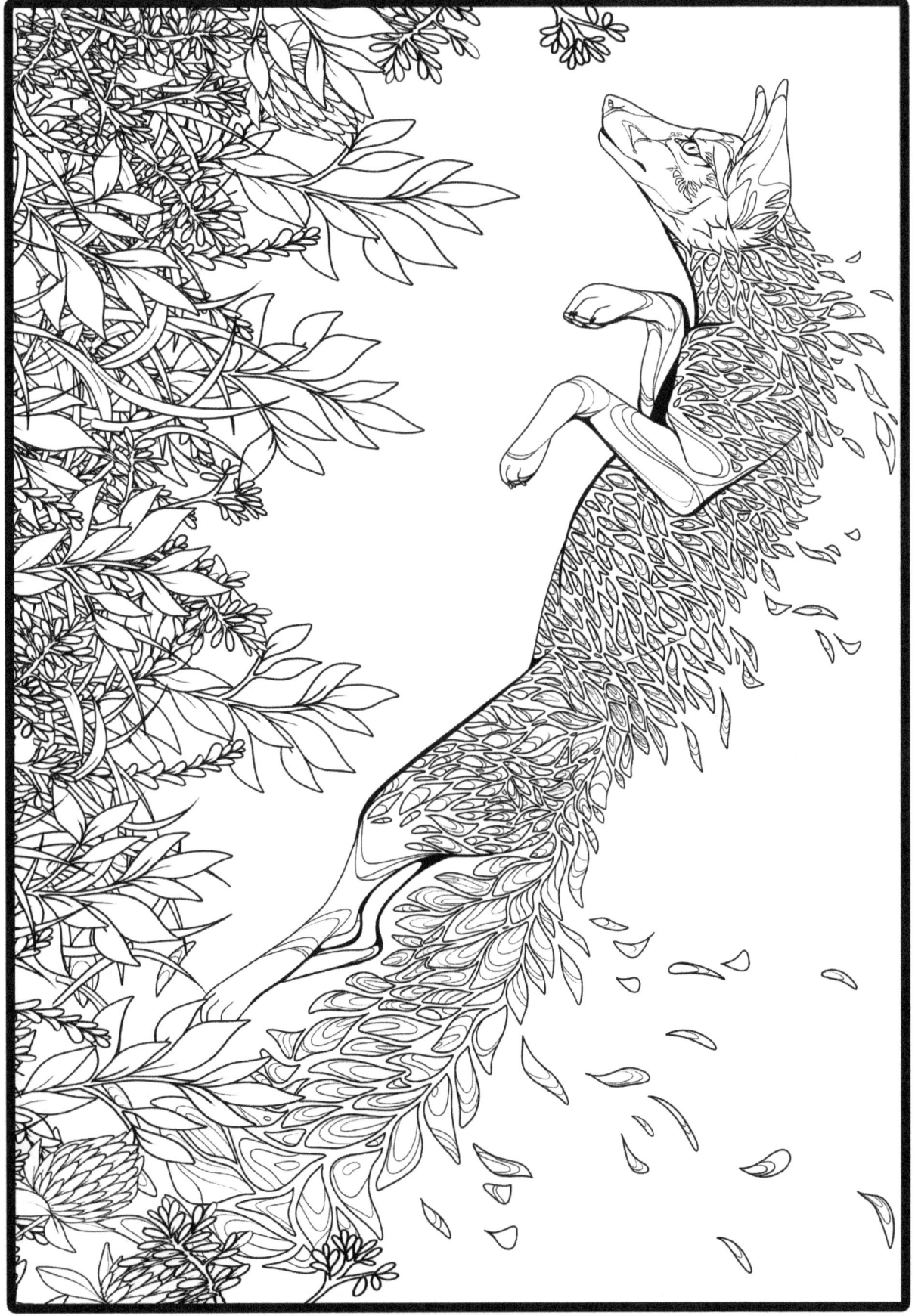

Bleed Page

This page exists to hopefully absorb any leakage of marker ink

Bleed Page

This page exists to hopefully absorb any leakage of marker ink

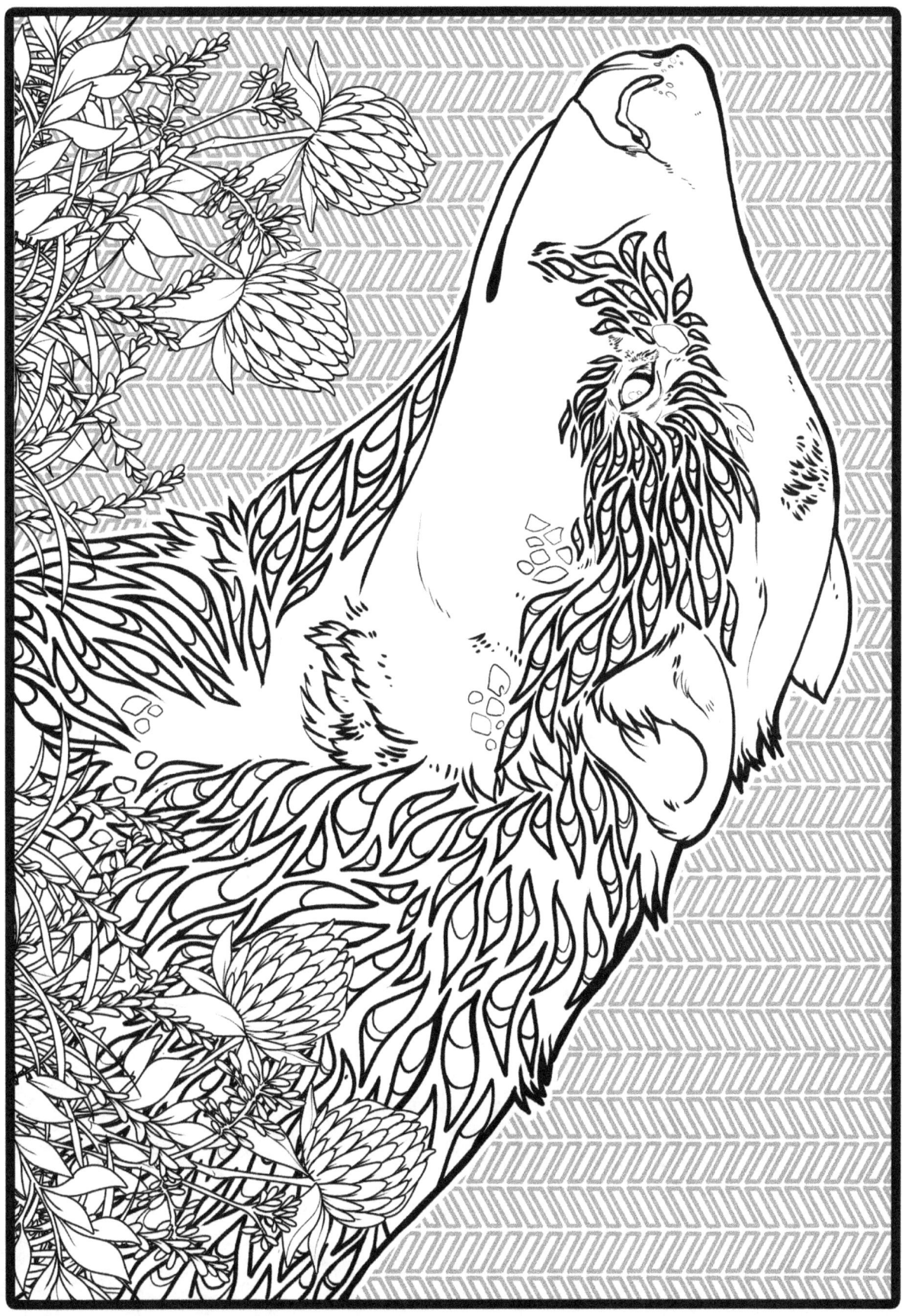

Bleed Page

This page exists to hopefully absorb any leakage of marker ink

Bleed Page

This page exists to hopefully absorb any leakage of marker ink

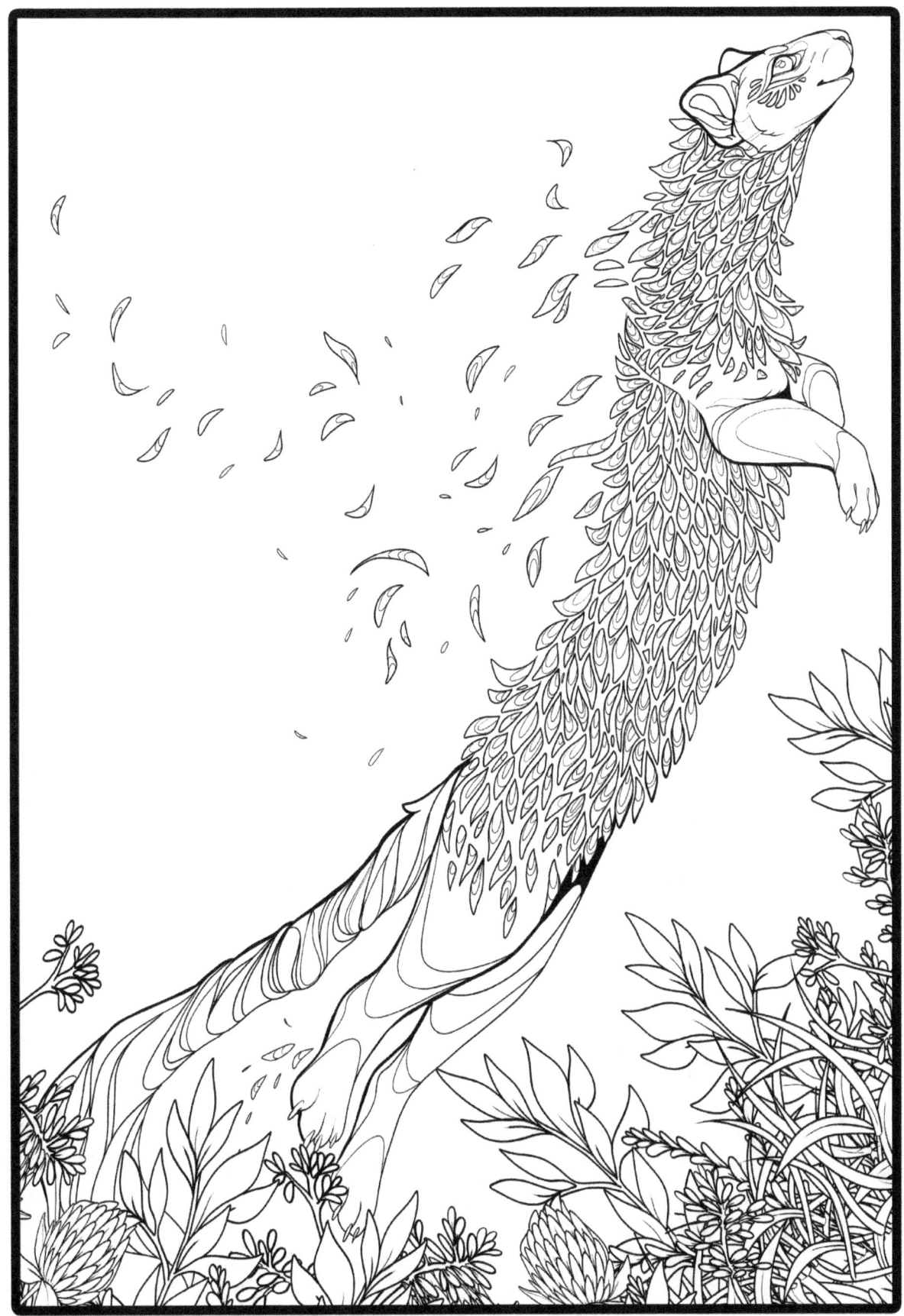

Bleed Page

This page exists to hopefully absorb any leakage of marker ink

Bleed Page

This page exists to hopefully absorb any leakage of marker ink

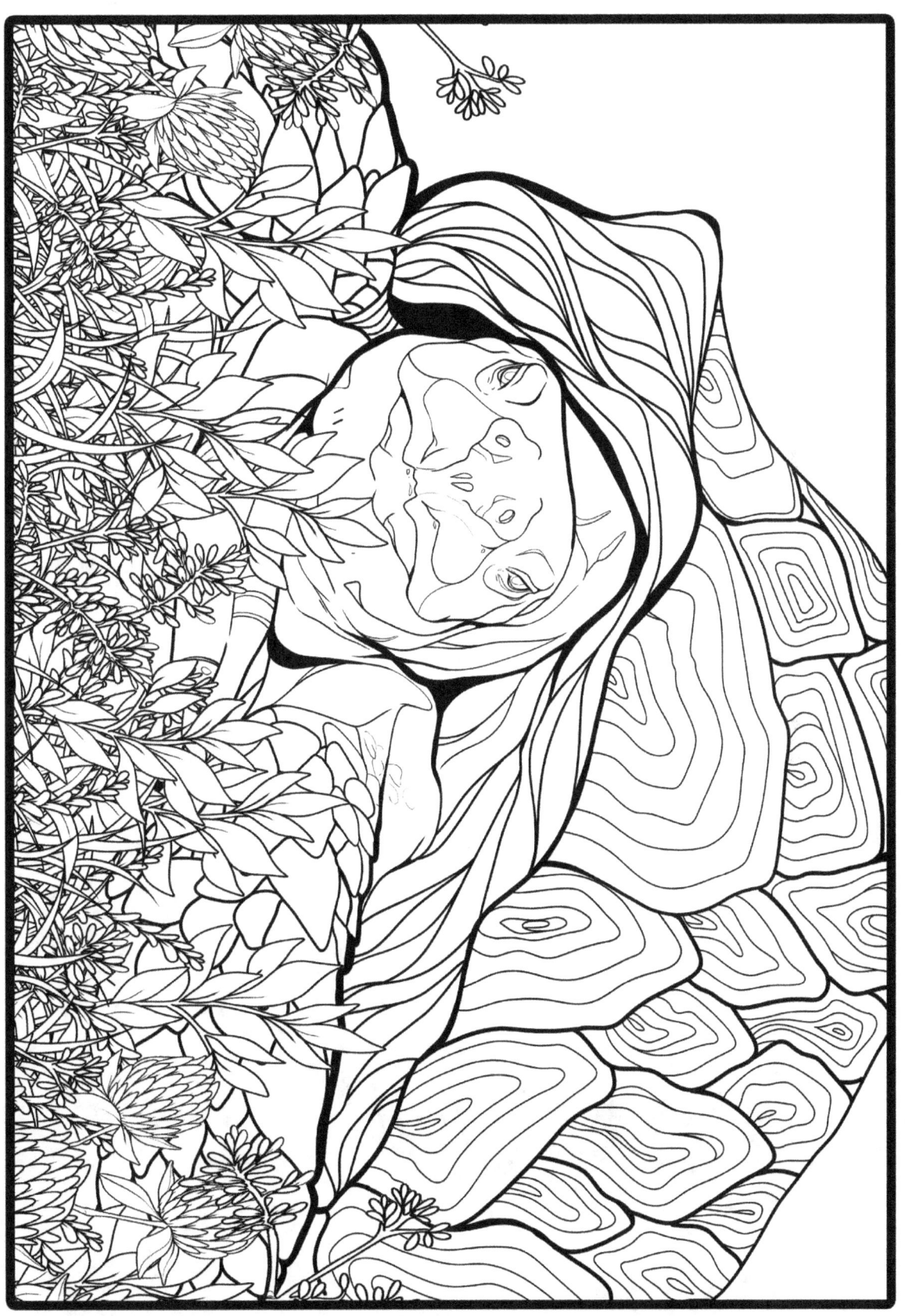

Bleed Page

This page exists to hopefully absorb any leakage of marker ink

Bleed Page

This page exists to hopefully absorb any leakage of marker ink

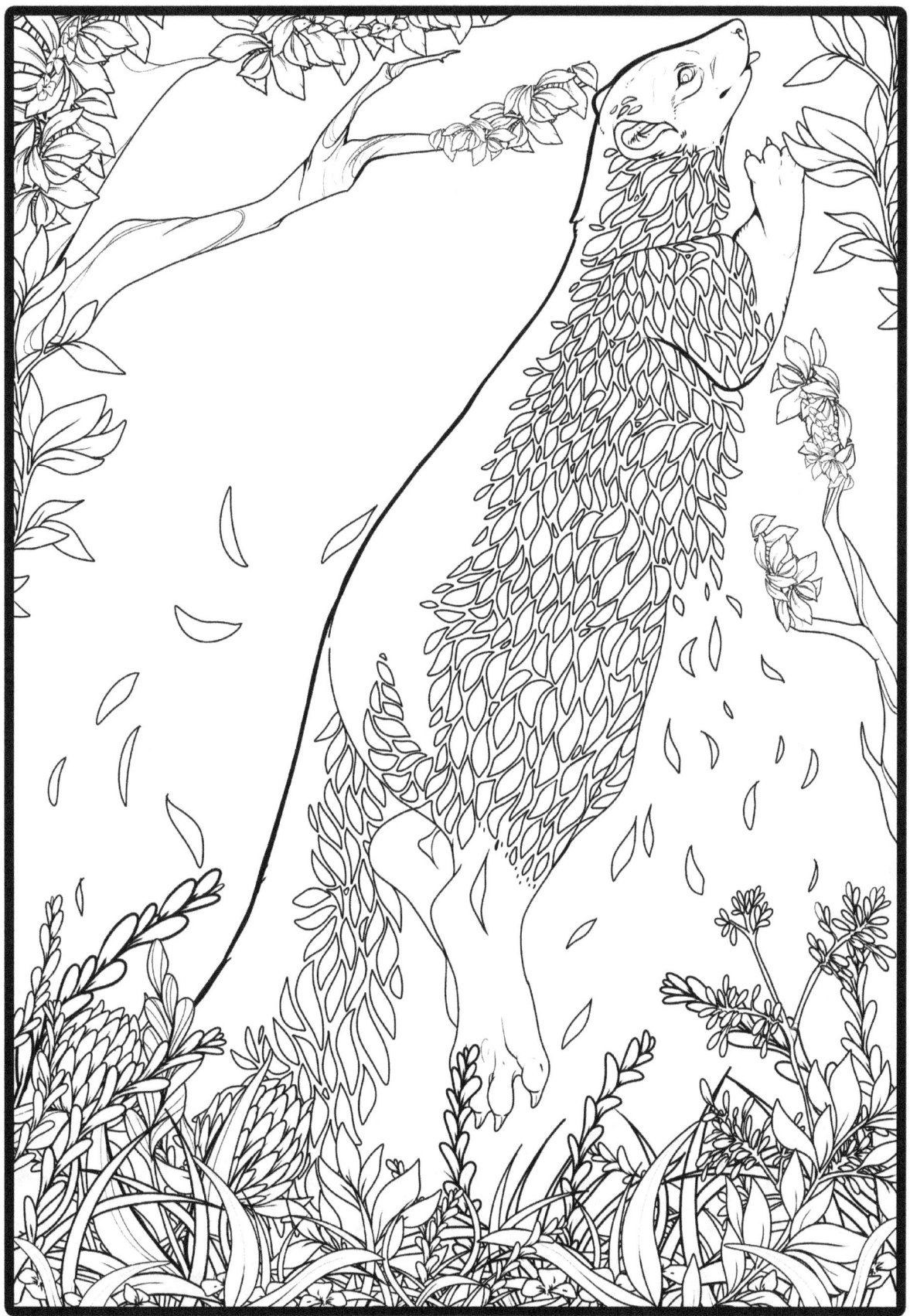

Bleed Page

This page exists to hopefully absorb any leakage of marker ink

Bleed Page

This page exists to hopefully absorb any leakage of marker ink

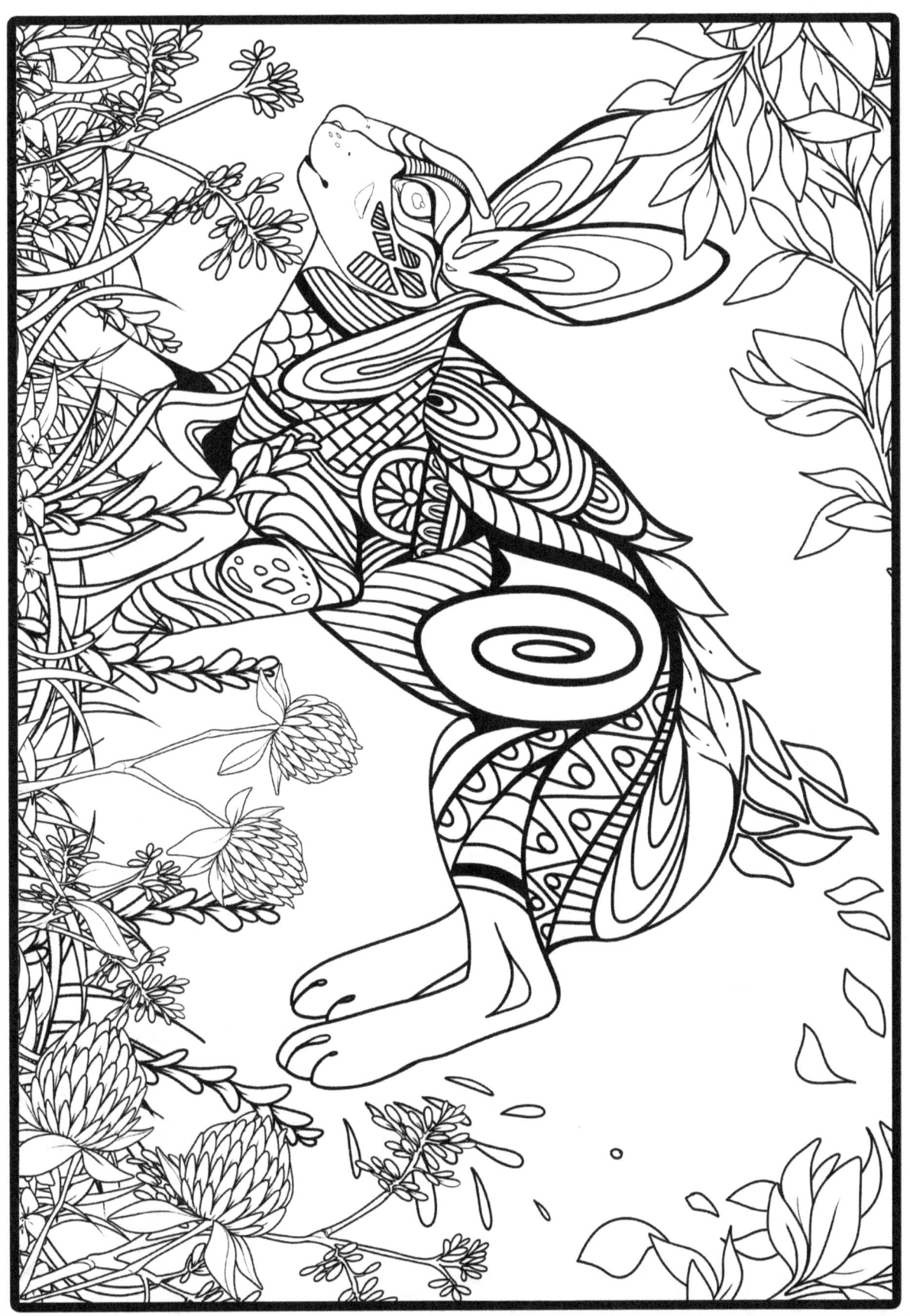

Bleed Page

This page exists to hopefully absorb any leakage of marker ink

Bleed Page

This page exists to hopefully absorb any leakage of marker ink

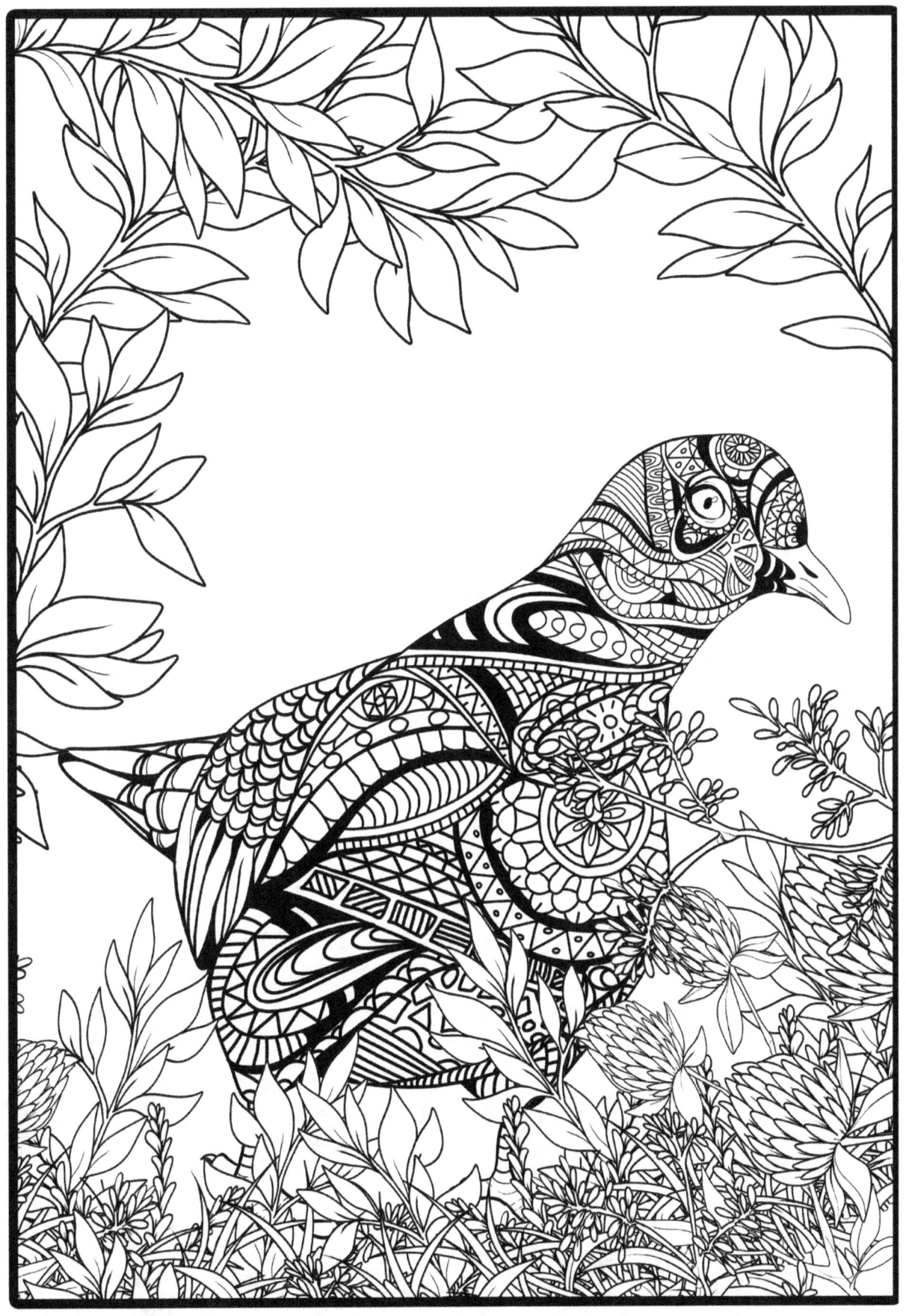

Bleed Page

This page exists to hopefully absorb any leakage of marker ink

Bleed Page

This page exists to hopefully absorb any leakage of marker ink

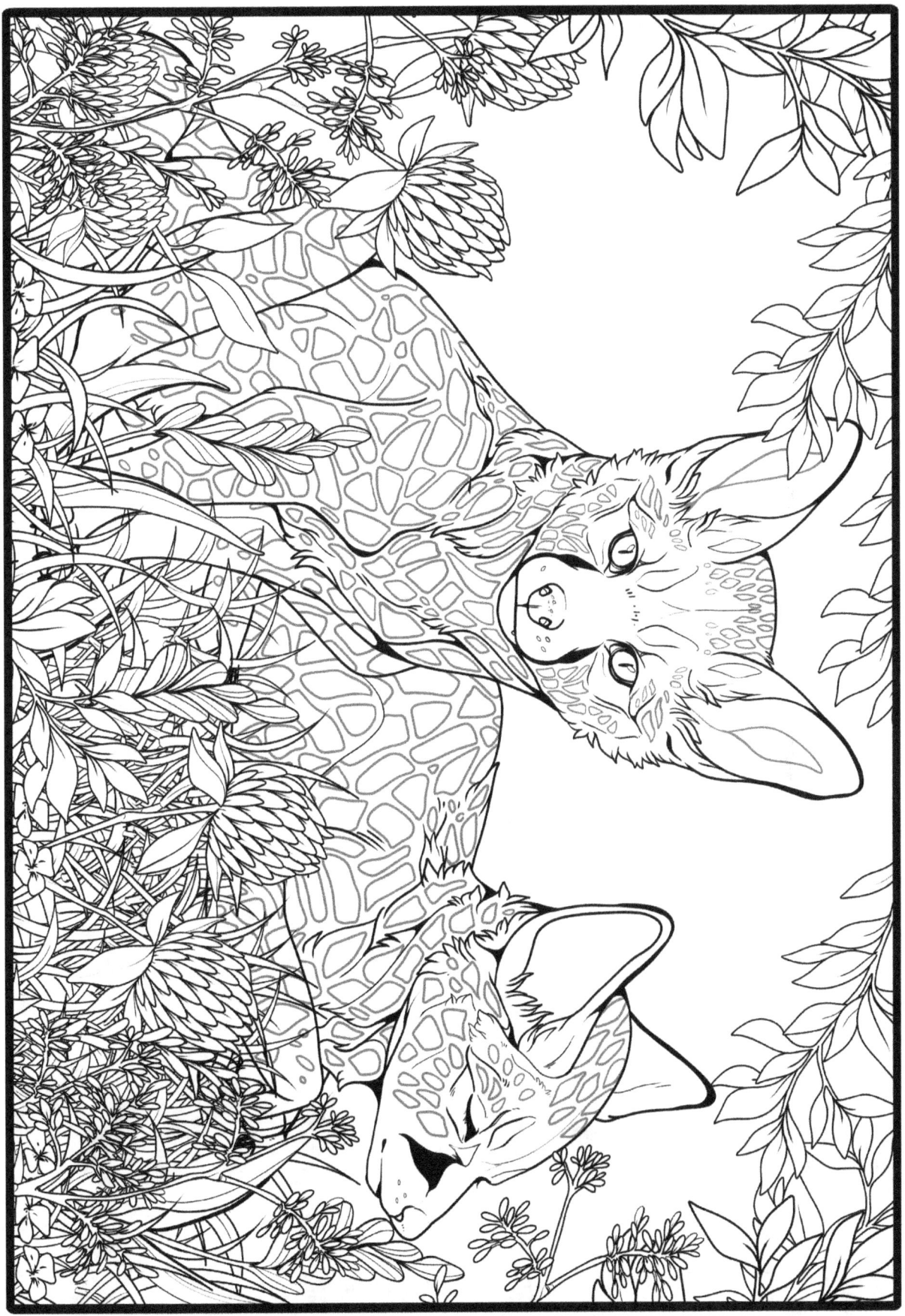

Bleed Page

This page exists to hopefully absorb any leakage of marker ink

Bleed Page

This page exists to hopefully absorb any leakage of marker ink

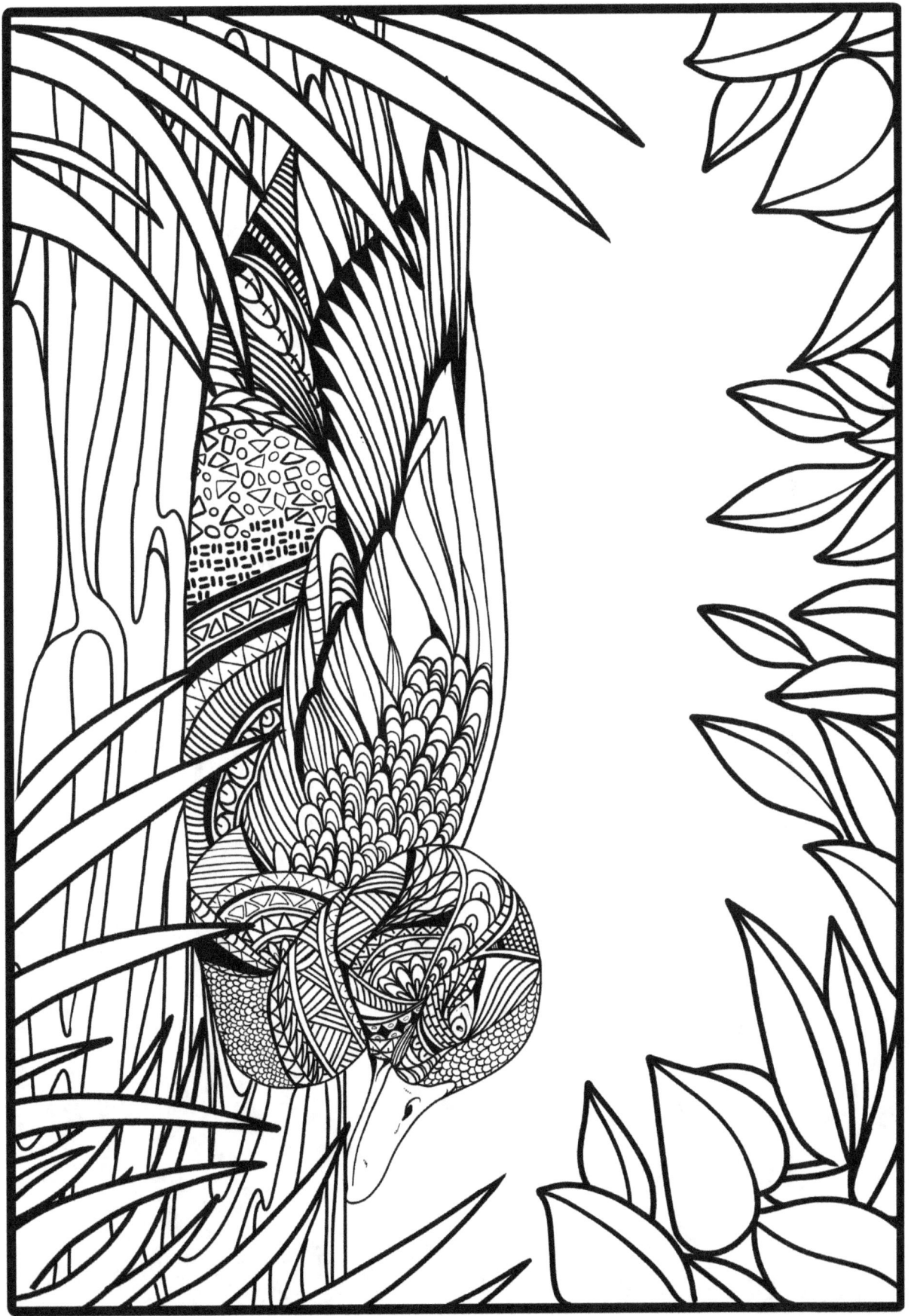

Bleed Page

This page exists to hopefully absorb any leakage of marker ink

Bleed Page

This page exists to hopefully absorb any leakage of marker ink

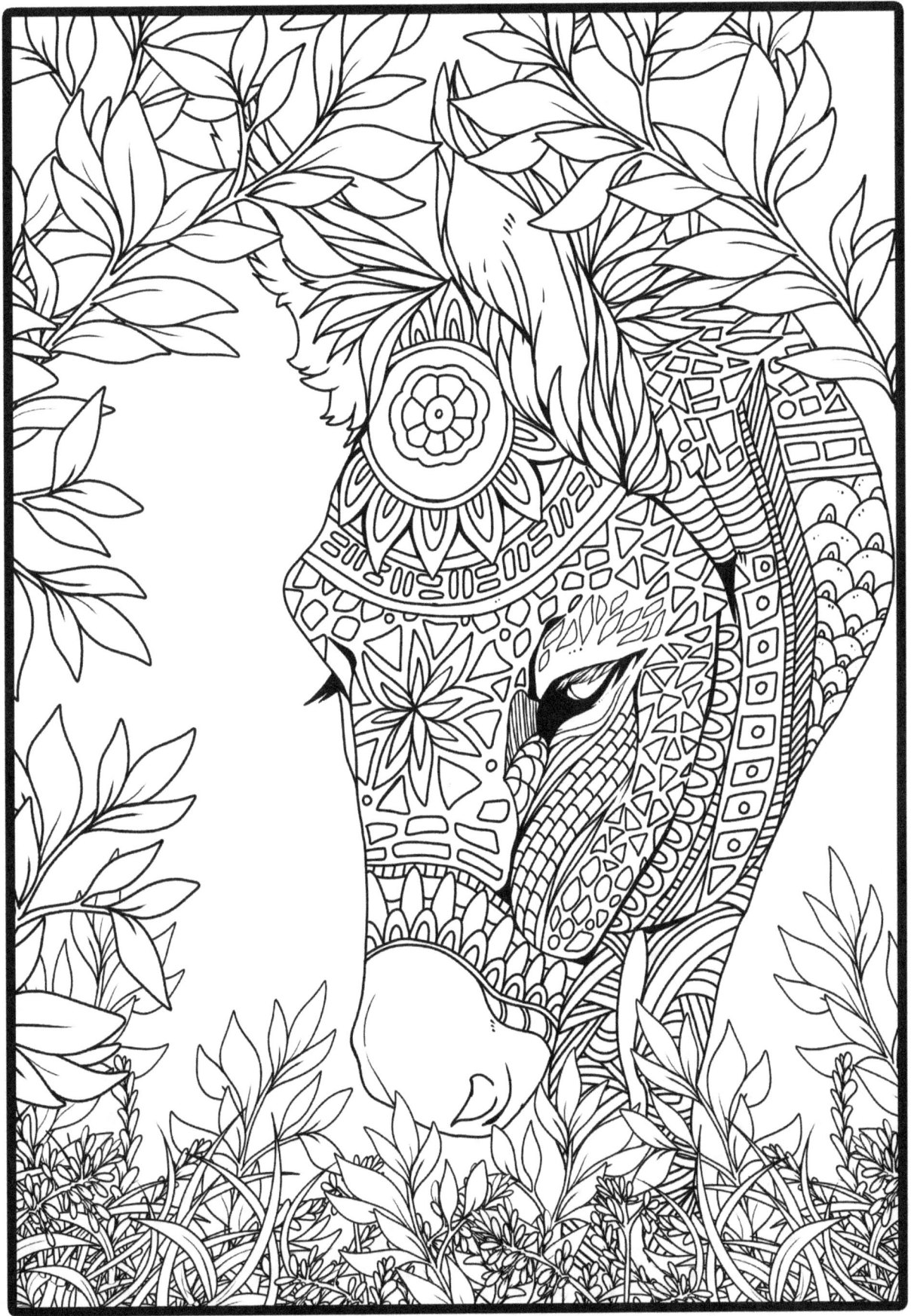

Bleed Page

This page exists to hopefully absorb any leakage of marker ink

Bleed Page

This page exists to hopefully absorb any leakage of marker ink

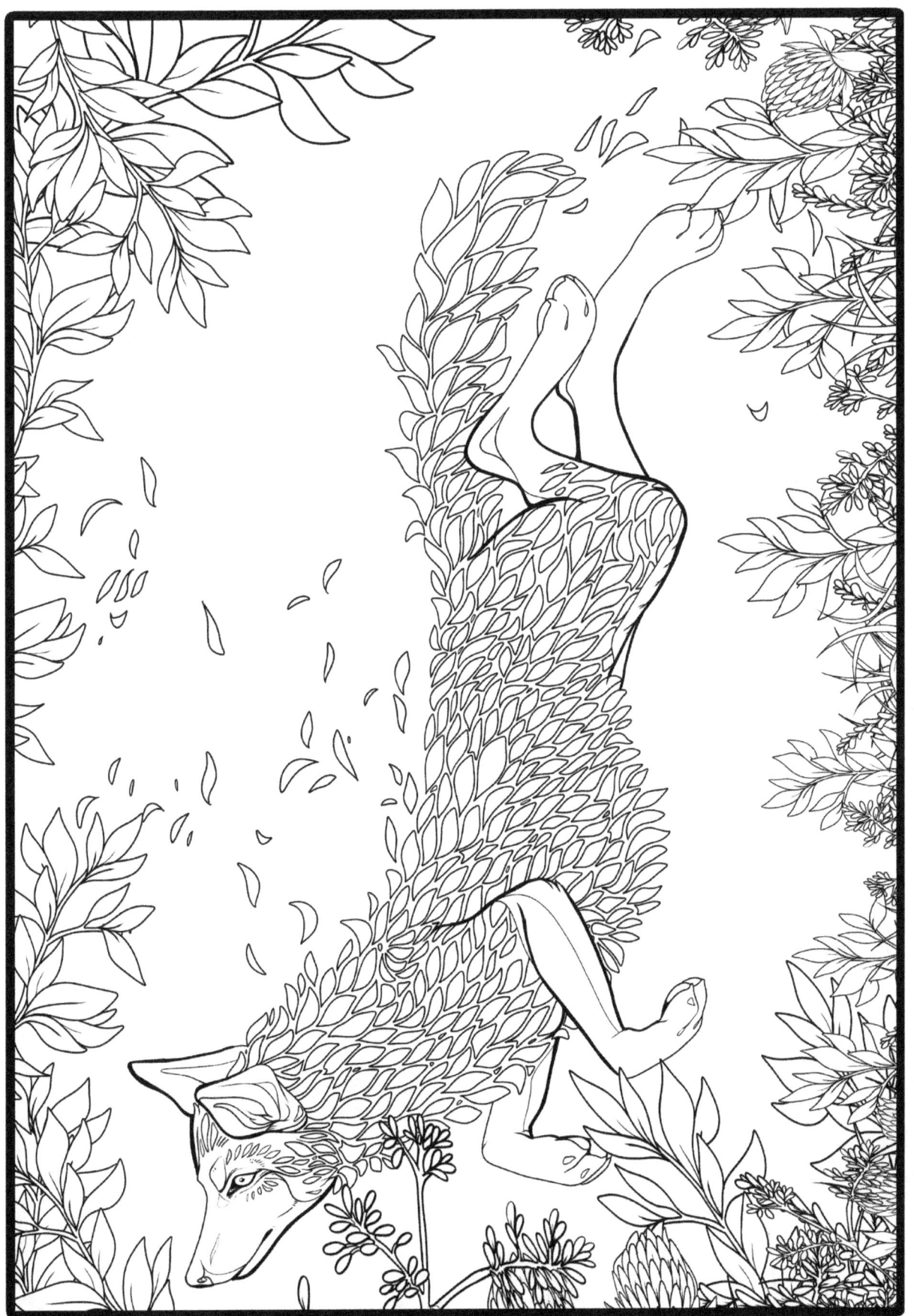

Bleed Page

This page exists to hopefully absorb any leakage of marker ink

Bleed Page

This page exists to hopefully absorb any leakage of marker ink

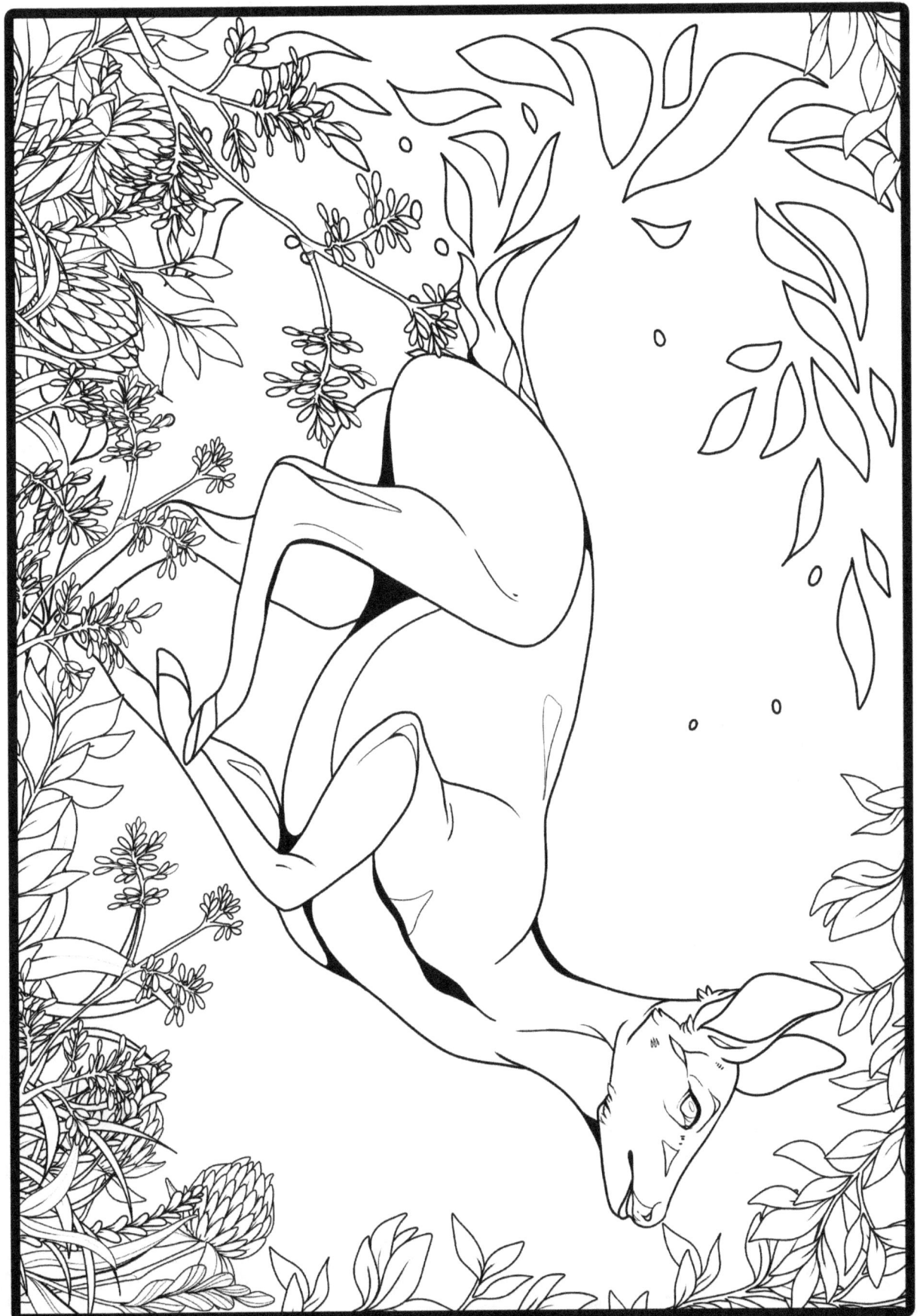

Bleed Page

This page exists to hopefully absorb any leakage of marker ink

Bleed Page

This page exists to hopefully absorb any leakage of marker ink

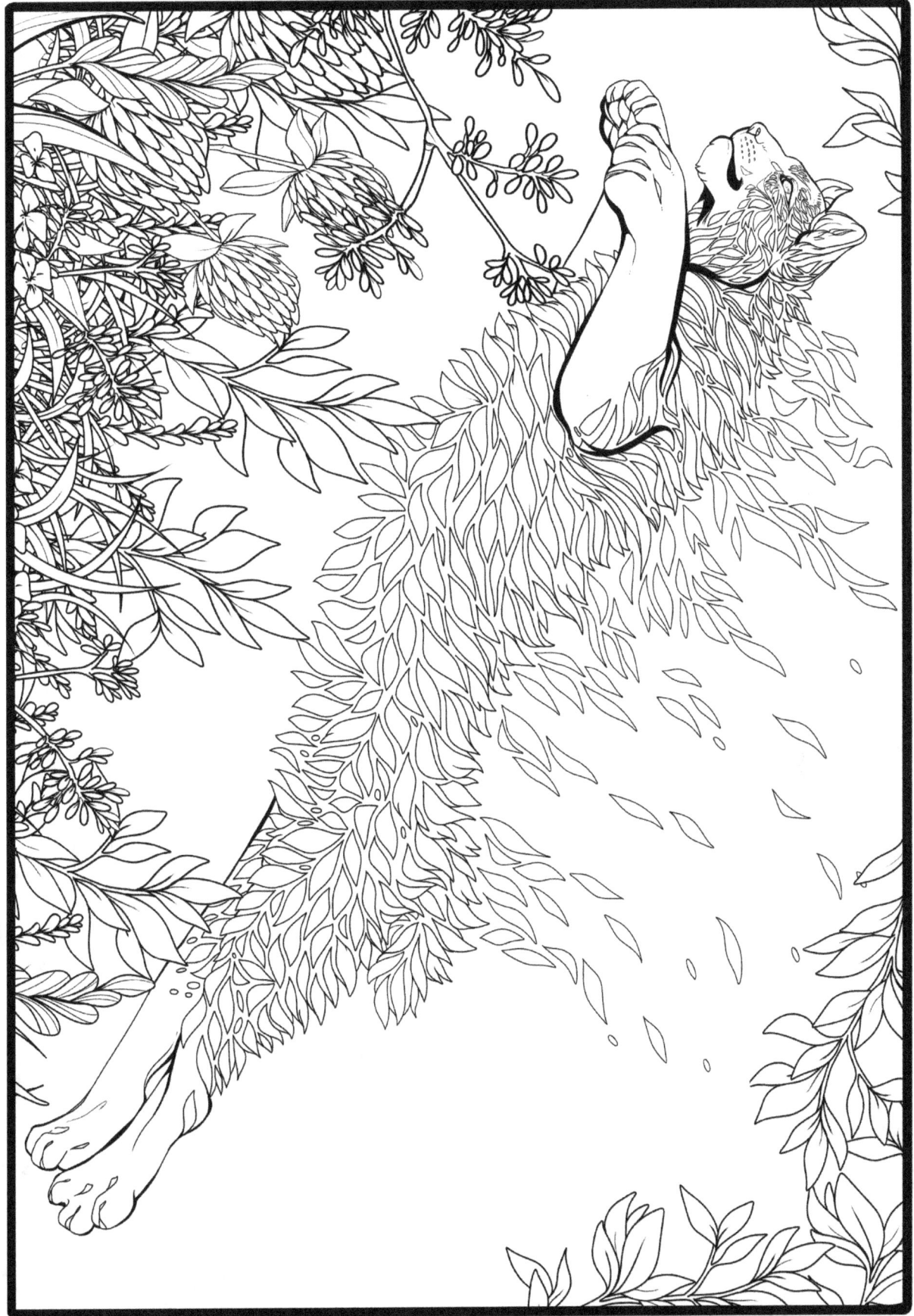

Bleed Page

This page exists to hopefully absorb any leakage of marker ink

Bleed Page

This page exists to hopefully absorb any leakage of marker ink

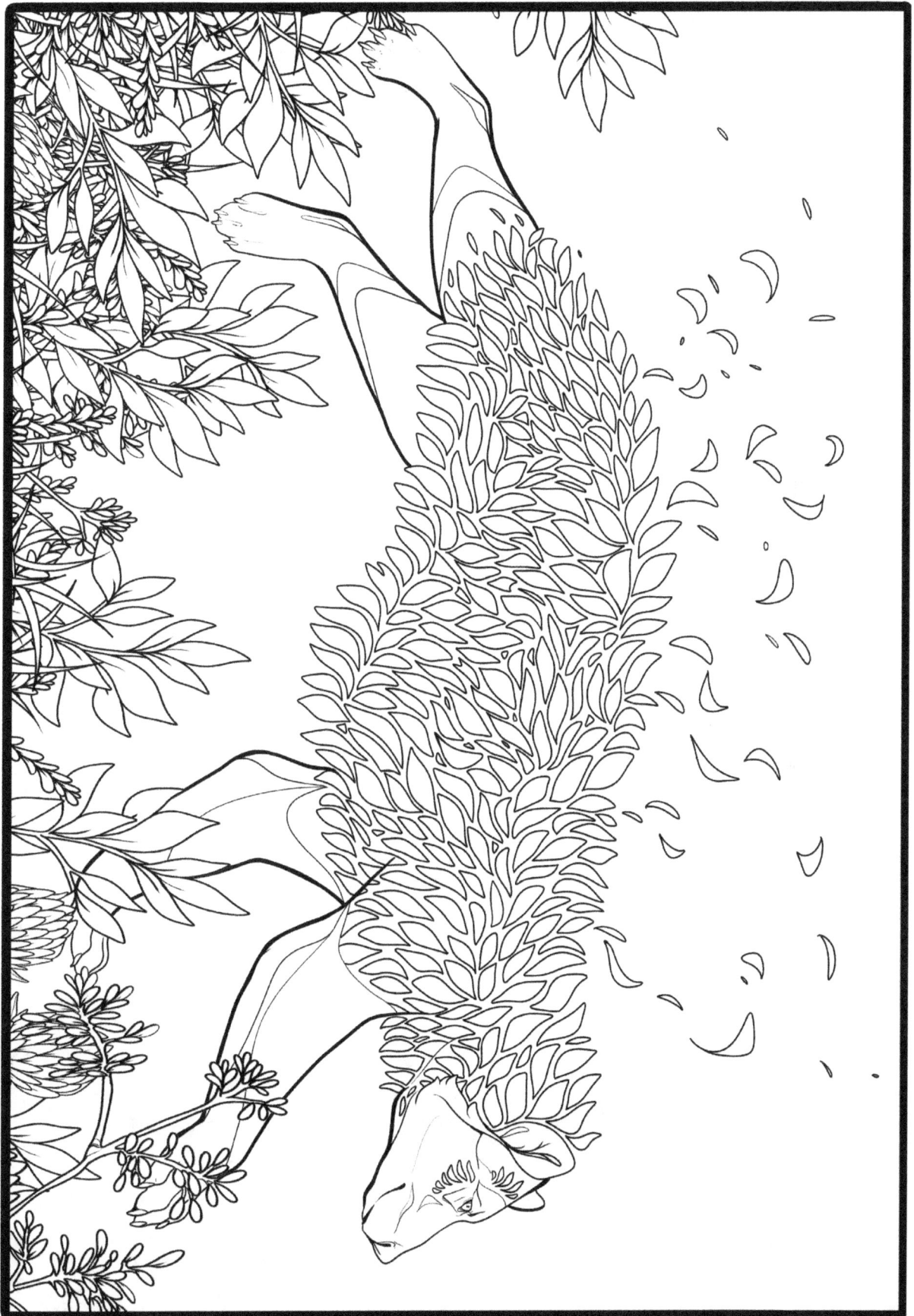

Bleed Page

This page exists to hopefully absorb any leakage of marker ink

Bleed Page

This page exists to hopefully absorb any leakage of marker ink

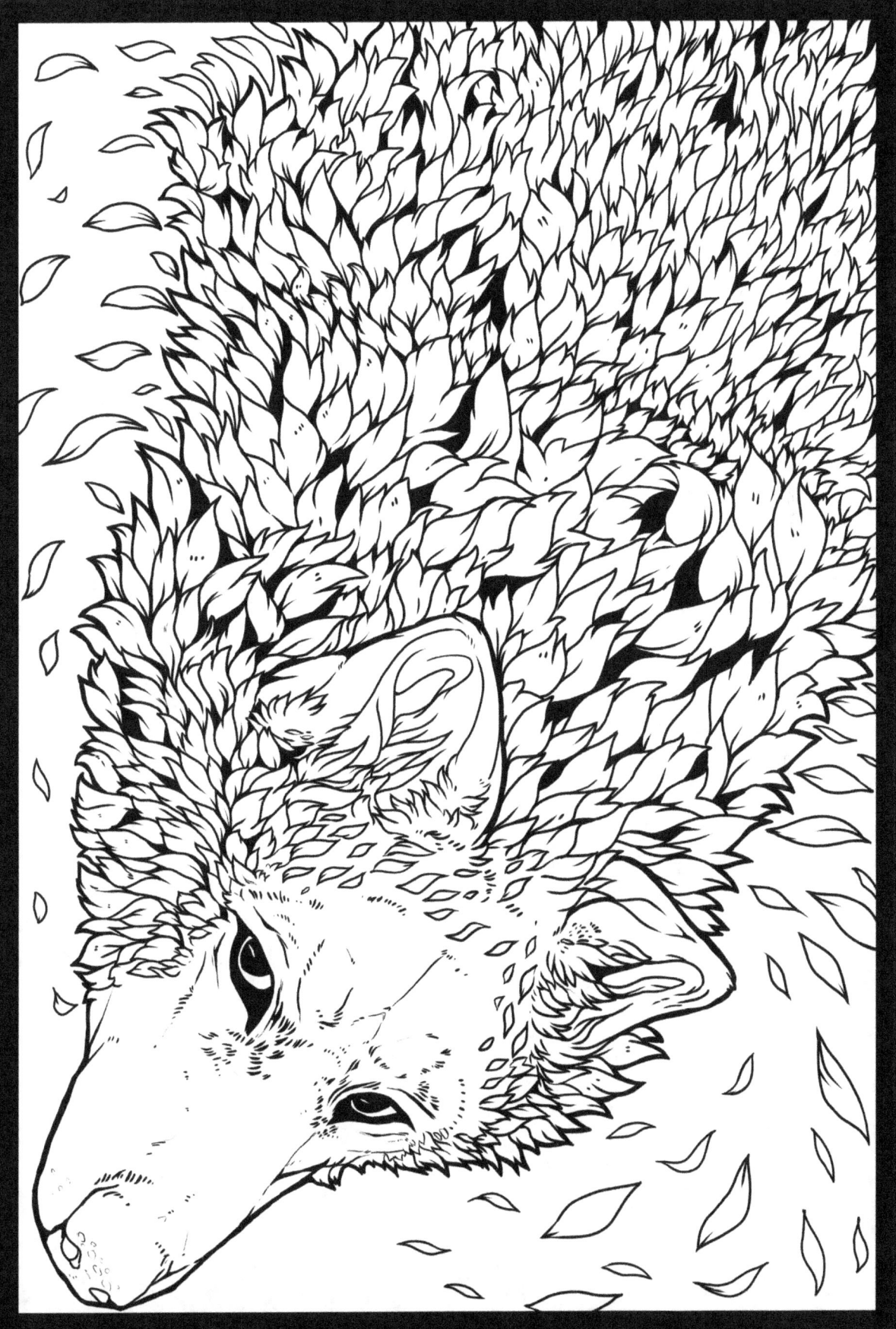

Bleed Page

This page exists to hopefully absorb any leakage of marker ink

Bleed Page

This page exists to hopefully absorb any leakage of marker ink

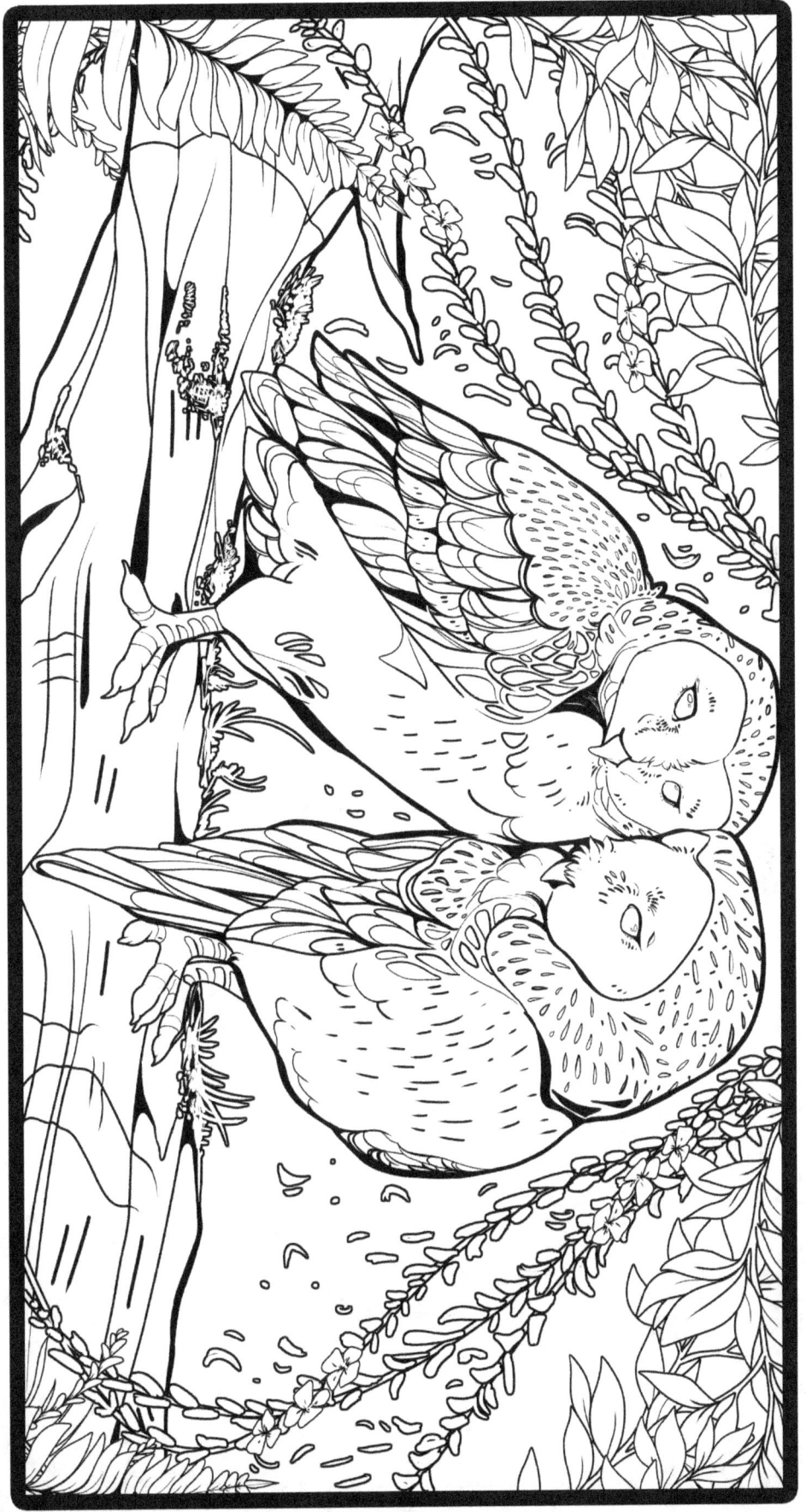

Bleed Page

This page exists to hopefully absorb any leakage of marker ink

Bleed Page

This page exists to hopefully absorb any leakage of marker ink

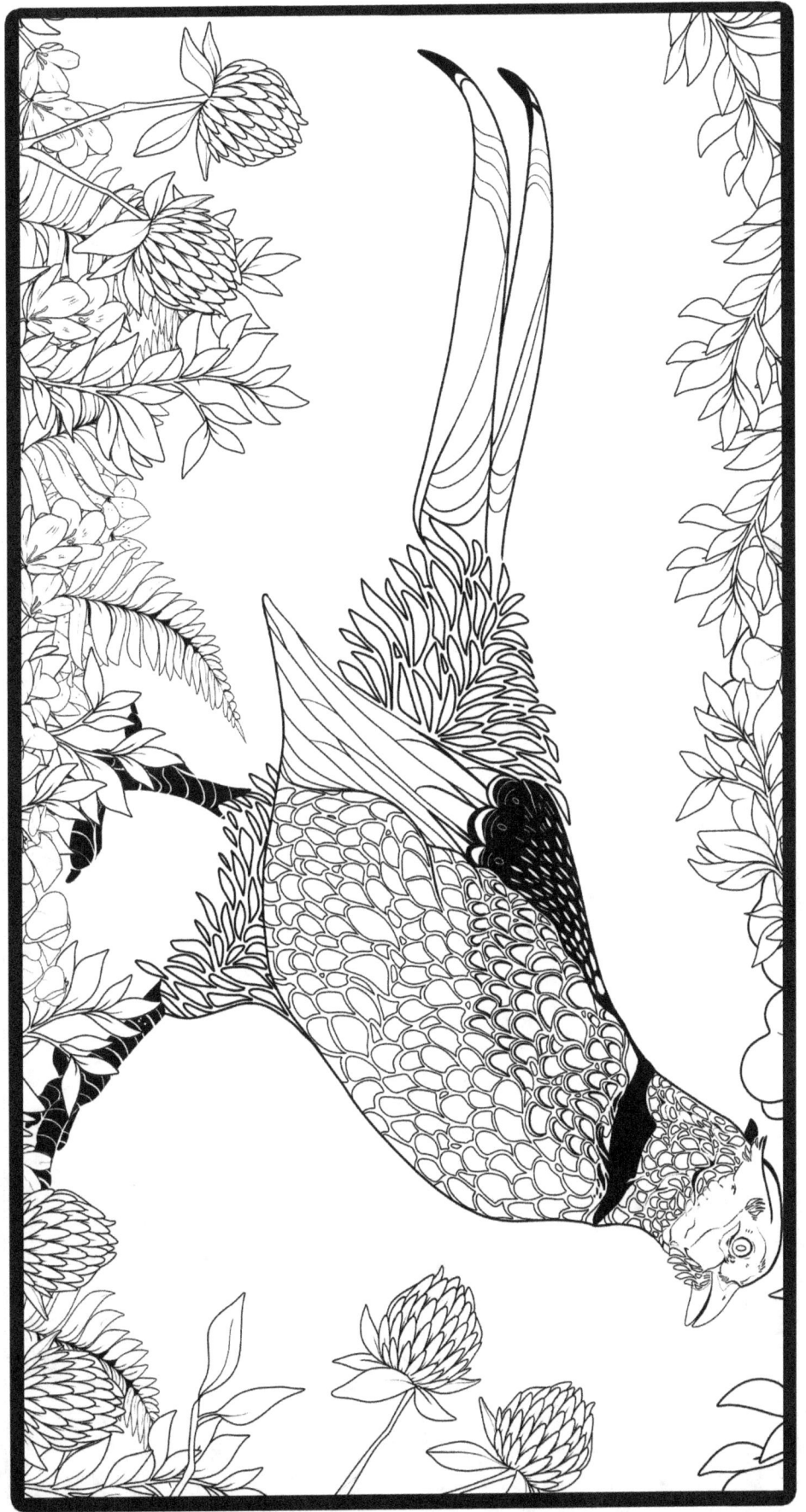

Bleed Page

This page exists to hopefully absorb any leakage of marker ink

Bleed Page

This page exists to
hopefully absorb any
leakage of marker ink

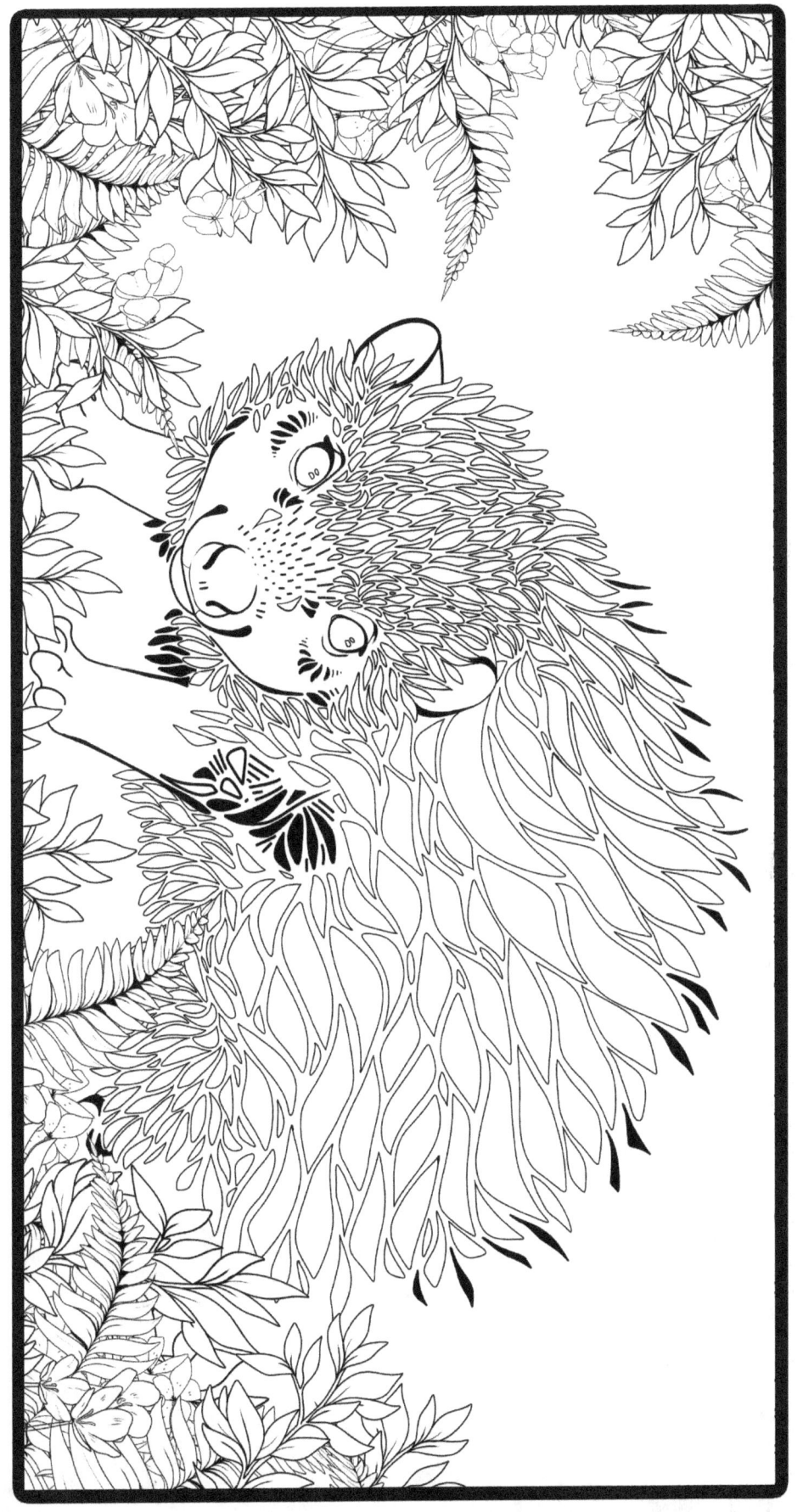

www.ingramcontent.com/pod-product-compliance
Lightning Source LLC
Chambersburg PA
CBHW080551220526
45466CB00010B/3118